Understanding China

For further volumes:
http://www.springer.com/series/11772

Hanyun Huang

Social Media Generation in Urban China

A Study of Social Media Use and Addiction among Adolescents

Springer

Dr. Hanyun Huang
School of Journalism and Communication
Xiamen University
Xiamen, People's Republic of China

ISSN 2196-3134 ISSN 2196-3142 (electronic)
ISBN 978-3-642-45440-0 ISBN 978-3-642-45441-7 (eBook)
DOI 10.1007/978-3-642-45441-7
Springer Heidelberg New York Dordrecht London

Library of Congress Control Number: 2013958450

Printed on acid-free paper

Springer is part of Springer Science+Business Media (www.springer.com)

To my dearest grandparents:
Seeing the fourth generation growing up
is the most wonderful thing in the world.

Acknowledgment

First, and most important, I would like to express my utmost gratitude to Prof. Louis Leung in the School of Journalism and Communication, the Chinese University of Hong Kong, for giving me the opportunity and leading me step by step into the academic world. Thank you so much, not only for giving this book the most patient and careful revision, but also for giving me a starting point of my academic life. Your rigorous research attitude, and your enthusiasm for students, set the best model for me as a researcher as well as a teacher.

My sincere thanks go to the Dean of the Faculty of Social Science, the Chinese University of Hong Kong, Prof. Paul Siu Nam Lee, for giving me lots of valuable guidance, support, and confidence during my years in CU; to Prof. Ven-hwei Lo in the School of Journalism and Communication, the Chinese University of Hong Kong, and to Prof. Cecilia Cheng in the Department of Psychology, University of Hong Kong, for providing me with many useful suggestions for improving this book.

I would also like to express my deep love to the Graduate School and School of Journalism and Communication, the Chinese University of Hong Kong. Thanks not only for sponsoring this research but also for giving me 5 years of peaceful and wonderful study time. You made me more grown up and become much stronger. I enjoyed every moment there. My gratitude also goes to the School of Journalism and Communication, Xiamen University, for giving me a perfect platform to start my academic career.

I am especially grateful to all the schools, directors, teachers, and adolescents who participated and supported this research. Thanks a lot for answering the questionnaire carefully and for willingly and openly coming forward to share your experience with me. It is your patience and courage that provided the foundation for this book.

Last but not least, special thanks go to my family—my four grandparents, my parents, my husband, and my lovely son—your love gave me the confidence and persistence to pursue this endeavor.

Acknowledgments

Contents

Abstract

Social media such as instant messaging (IM), social networking sites (SNS), blogs, and microblogs are heavily immersed into adolescents' lives in China. Anecdotal evidence reported in the news suggested that the increasing popularity of social media could make adolescents more vulnerable to being addicted. This exploratory study proposes the concept of "social media addiction" and examines (a) whether social media addiction exists among adolescents in urban China and, if so, who the addicts are, what their symptoms are, and to what extent they are addicted; (b) whether sociopsychological traits (e.g., need for affiliation, impression management, narcissism, and leisure boredom) can predict social media addiction among adolescents; (c) what gratifications are obtained by adolescents from their use of social media and whether these gratifications can predict social media addiction; and (d) to what degree social media addiction influences adolescents' academic performance and social capital.

This study adopted quantitative questionnaire surveys among adolescents as the main research method, supplemented by qualitative pre-survey focus groups among adolescents and post-survey in-depth interviews among parents and teachers. Questionnaire surveys were conducted based on a multistage cluster sampling of seven middle schools in five urban Chinese cities: Beijing, Shanghai, Guangzhou, Shenzhen, and Xiamen. The final sample consisted of 1,549 adolescents, of whom 90 % had used social media. Using Young's classic definition of Internet addiction, 15.6 % of participants were classified as social media addicts. The addicted adolescents were often self-absorbed, leisurely bored, and good at manipulation through social media for impression management. Addicts experienced four major social media addiction symptoms: preoccupation, adverse consequences, alleviation of negative emotions, and loss of interest in social activities.

The seven social media gratifications identified in this study can be categorized into social, information, and entertainment gratifications. Among these, entertainment gratifications had the most power to predict social media addiction, while information gratifications were the least likely to lead to addiction. Furthermore, these gratifications were found to be powerful mediators between the adolescents' sociopsychological traits and social media addiction. Finally, results also indicated that social media addiction, particularly its symptoms, had significant negative impact on adolescents' academic performance and social capital.

List of Figures

List of Tables

Chapter 1
Introduction

1.1 Background

China has the largest netizen population in the world. At the end of 2010, there were 457 million Internet users in China, of which 27.3 % were between the ages of 10 and 19 (China Internet Network Information Center-CNNIC 2011). According to the "2009 Research Report of China Youth Internet Behaviors" published in April, 2010, by CNNIC, adolescents were very active in online communication. On average, they spent 12.1 h online every week. Instant messenger (IM), blogs, and social network sites (SNS) were the three most popular online communication applications among adolescents in middle schools (grades 7–12), and the proportions of use for these applications (approximated by the number of adolescents participated in specific application divided by the total number of adolescent Internet users) were 80.5 %, 69.5 %, and 40.1 %, respectively. It is remarkable that the proportions of IM and blog use were much higher among adolescents than among netizens in general (CNNIC 2010). This indicates that social media is becoming increasingly popular and penetrating deeply into the lives of adolescents in China.

Going beyond being popular among adolescents in China, social media have now evolved into a much-debated public concern due to excessive and maladaptive use. Anecdotal news reports provided evidence that the increasing popularity of social media might have made adolescents more vulnerable to addiction. Some anecdotes include the following:

- A 17-year-old boy committed suicide when his net girlfriend, whom he had met and contacted through IM for more than 10 h a day, refused to meet him in real life and suddenly disappeared (Liu and Ma 2011).
- Another boy committed suicide after he found out that his lover online through IM for 2 years was a middle-aged housewife (Xinhua News Agency 2006).
- A 15-year-old girl skipped classes and was found in an Internet café chatting with her male net friend through IM for 2 days and nights, and later ran away from home with him in real life (Gu 2007).

H. Huang, *Social Media Generation in Urban China: A Study of Social Media Use and Addiction among Adolescents*, Understanding China,
DOI 10.1007/978-3-642-45441-7_1, © Springer-Verlag Berlin Heidelberg 2014

- A boy wanted to chat with his net friend in an Internet café, so he climbed over the wall of his boarding school at night (Yang et al. 2002).
- Some middle-school students set their alarm clocks to get up in the middle of the night to "steal vegetables" in the SNS game, "Happy Farm," and then could not concentrate in class because they were worried that their ripe vegetables would be stolen by others (Zhuang and Ai 2010).

Bestsellers also focus on discussing the excessive use of social media among adolescents. For example, in his latest book, *The Dumbest Generation*, Mark Bauerlein (2008) pointed out that the current "MySpace generation" has become the dumbest generation because they spend too much time on social media like SNS and IM. They do not study and read enough, so their knowledge, reading ability, social responsibility, and capacity to compete internationally could not match the abilities of previous generations (Bauerlein 2008). This study is motivated by the above evidence that popular but excessive use of social media may have significant negative impact on adolescents.

In recent years, increasingly more news reports in China have pointed out that Internet addiction is a "severe social problem that could threaten the nation's future" (Fallows 2007). In 2010, the China Youth Internet Association (CYIA) and the Communication University of China jointly published the "China Youth Internet Addiction Report 2009." The report showed that among adolescents between 13 and 17 years old, 14.3 % were addicted to the Internet. Among these adolescent Internet addicts, half were addicted to online games (CYIA 2010). Results of the joint report show that Internet addiction has impaired adolescents' academic performance. Furthermore, Internet-addicted adolescents consistently could not get along well with their peers and teachers (CYIA 2010).

Previous academic research has investigated Internet addiction among Chinese adolescents from various perspectives using different research questions and hypotheses (Cao and Su 2007; Chak and Leung 2004; Cheung and Wong 2011; Geng et al. 2006; Gong et al. 2009; Ko et al. 2007, 2008; Lam et al. 2009; Li et al. 2006; Liu 2007; Tsai and Lin 2003; Yang and Tung 2007). However, most of these studies discussed Internet addiction as a general phenomenon or emphasized online game addiction among adolescents but largely ignored whether the excessive use of online interpersonal communication can also lead to addiction. Given the popularity of various kinds of social media among Chinese adolescents, social media are very attractive and capable of making adolescents overly indulge in online interpersonal communications, which places them in danger of becoming addicts.

To date, there has been little research on whether use of social media is addictive or dependence forming. Therefore, this study proposes "social media addiction" as a concept for further investigation. This study is one of the first to test empirically and demonstrate that social media addiction indeed exists among adolescents in China, to which parents and teachers should pay attention. Meanwhile, this study goes beyond examining the level of addiction and tries to identify the symptoms of social media addiction that adolescents experience.

Knowledge of these symptoms can help parents and educators detect and assess social media addiction among adolescents in order to intervene appropriately at an early stage.

1.2 Theoretical Framework of the Study

The approach of uses and gratifications (U&G) has long been used to study how people use media. Katz et al. (1974) described the U&G approach to media studies as "(1) the social and psychological origins of (2) needs, which generate (3) expectations of (4) the mass media and other sources, which lead to (5) differential patterns of media exposure, resulting in (6) need gratifications and (7) other consequences, perhaps mostly unintended ones" (p. 20). This study adopts the U&G approach to identify the social and psychological origins of social media use among adolescents in urban China, which lead to differential patterns of their social media use, resulting in gratifications and potential social media addiction, and other possible consequences such as decreases in academic performance and social capital. This study also identifies unique gratifications that emphasize the "social" features of social media.

Previous research has examined the psychological antecedents of Internet addiction such as shyness (Chak and Leung 2004; Huang and Leung 2009; Yuen and Lavin 2004), loneliness (Ghassemzadeh et al. 2008; Nalwa and Anand 2003; Odaci and Kalkan 2010), alienation (Huang and Leung 2009), self-esteem (Ghassemzadeh et al. 2008; Ko et al. 2007), and depression (Cheung and Wong 2011; Tsai and Lin 2003). To emphasize the social features of social media, this study explores further the social antecedents that may be responsible for triggering social media addiction. Based on the previous literature and suggested by the results of focus groups, this study investigates potential predictors of social media addiction, particularly the social dimension of personality traits (i.e., the need for affiliation and impression management) and the psychological dimension of personality traits (i.e., narcissism and leisure boredom).

Past research indicated that the need for affiliation not only makes people actively involved in offline activities but also motivates them to participate in various online activities (Gibbs et al. 2006). For some users, having full control over the information they publish online is extremely important; and impression management in online communication can be longer term, more strategic, effective, and systematic than in face-to-face self-presentations (Leary 1996; Kramer and Winter 2008). When packaging one's personal profiles at SNS such as Facebook, the possibilities of including more self-promoting contents and more attractive photos for inflated affirmations, as well as updating profile pictures and status frequently, are reasons attracting narcissistic youth to patronize SNS (Buffardi and Campbell 2008; Correa et al. 2010). Previous studies also showed that adolescents who were bored during their leisure time tended to be addicted to both the

Internet (Lin et al. 2009) and the mobile phones (Leung 2008). This study expands the existing literature to investigate further how these social and psychological traits can predict adolescents' social media addiction.

Parents and educators are eager to know the impact of social media on adolescents' lives. Previous studies suggested that Internet use has negative effects on adolescents' academic performance. Some scholars remained optimistic, however, and proposed that if adolescents used the Internet for online learning or group discussions, the effects could be positive (Cheuk and Chan 2007). Previous findings on Internet use and social capital are also diverse. Some scholars believe that Internet use promotes social capital, and others suggest that Internet use can diminish social capital; still others reveal that Internet use reinforces offline interactions and supplements the development of social capital (Ellison et al. 2010). To provide a more conclusive and comprehensive understanding of social media addiction, this study further investigates the impact of social media use from a Chinese perspective, focusing on urban Chinese adolescents.

1.3 Research Objectives

As a whole, this exploratory research proposes "social media addiction" as a concept for study. Specifically, this research examines (a) whether social media addiction exists among adolescents in urban China and, if so, who the addicts are, what their symptoms are, and to what extent they are addicted; (b) whether sociopsychological traits such as need for affiliation, impression management, narcissism, and leisure boredom can predict social media addiction; (c) what gratifications adolescents obtain from using social media and whether these gratifications can predict social media addiction; and (d) whether and to what degree social media addiction influences adolescents' academic performance and social capital.

This study attempts to fill the gap in previous media addiction researches that were mostly from western perspectives. The study aims to contribute to both theory and practice. In theory, this study adopts the U&G approach to enrich the scope of media addiction research. This study is also in line with the media effects tradition by exploring the possible influence of the new media on people in terms of satisfying their social and psychological needs and the possible negative effects due to heavy use of the media. In practice, this study cautions parents and educators the existence of social media addiction among adolescents is real, not only in China but also possible in other developed countries around the world, and such addiction can impair adolescents' academic performance and social capital. Parents and educators can use the symptoms as early warning signs to detect social media addiction among adolescents, so that they can provide appropriate guidance and preventions at an early stage of the problem.

1.4 Research Methods

To achieve the above research objectives, this study adopted a combination of both quantitative and qualitative research methods.

It is well known that there are major differences between urban cities and suburban or rural areas in China. Adolescents in remote districts may not even have access to the Internet, not to mention social media. As an exploratory study, multiple theoretical constructs and important sociopsychological variables were adopted to assess, predict, and explain the latest status of social media addiction among adolescents from five developed urban cities in China—Beijing, Shanghai, Guangzhou, Shenzhen, and Xiamen.

Survey as the main method was executed among a multistage cluster sampling of adolescents from middle schools in the five major metropolitan areas. Before the survey, focus groups among adolescents were held to assist research conceptualization and questionnaire design. After the survey, in-depth interviews were conducted with the adolescents' parents and teachers. As supplements to the survey results, the in-depth interviews provided a comprehensive understanding of the status of social media addiction among adolescents.

1.5 Main Contents of Each Chapter

This dissertation consists of eight chapters. After this introduction chapter, Chap. 2 reviews the previous literature on social media and their penetration in China; U&G studies, from history to the latest studies on social media; Internet addiction research; sociopsychological traits (i.e., the need for affiliation, impression management, narcissism, and leisure boredom) and their relationships with Internet and social media use and addiction; and the effects of Internet and social media on adolescents' academic performance and social capital. Grounded in previous literature, hypotheses are proposed and research questions are raised.

Chapter 3 introduces the research methods and measurements used in this study. Survey as the main research method is discussed in detail about survey participants, pilot test, sampling procedure, the process of data collection, final sample profiles, operational definition of variables, reliability of the scales, and analytical procedures. The focus groups and in-depth interviews are also addressed.

Chapters 4, 5, and 6 present the findings of the survey. Specifically, Chap. 4 discusses social media addiction among adolescents in urban China from the U&G perspective; Chap. 5 focuses on examining social media addiction among adolescents in urban China based on the effects of sociopsychological traits; Chap. 6 explores the impact of social media addiction on adolescents' academic performance and social capital.

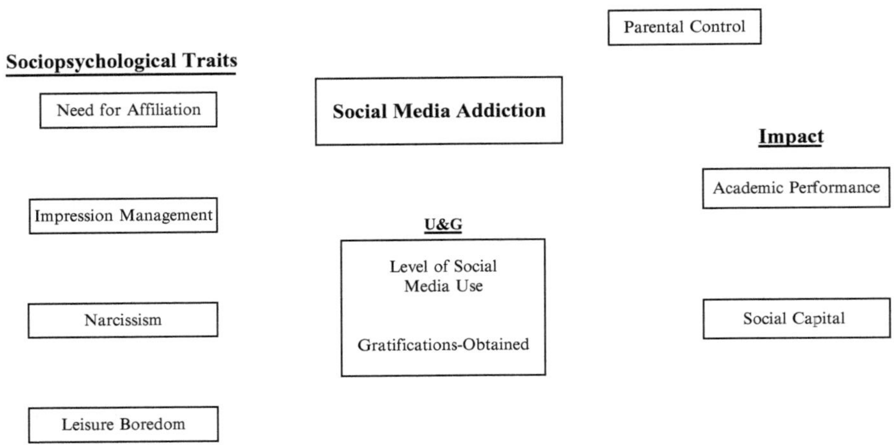

Fig. 1.1 Conceptual framework

Chapter 7 discusses the qualitative data from in-depth interviews of parents and teachers, during which they discuss their concerns and worries about adolescents' social media addiction. This chapter supplements the survey results.

Finally, Chap. 8 discusses the important findings of this research and makes conclusions. It also elaborates the theoretical contributions and practical implications of this study. The limitations of this study and suggestions for future research are also addressed.

Figure 1.1 presents the conceptual framework for this study.

References

Bauerlein, M. (2008). *The dumbest generation: How the digital age stupefies young Americans and jeopardizes our future*. New York: Penguin Group.

Buffardi, L. E., & Campbell, W. K. (2008). Narcissism and social networking websites. *Personality and Social Psychology Bulletin, 34*, 1303–1314.

Cao, F., & Su, L. (2007). Internet addiction among Chinese adolescents: Prevalence and psychological features. *Child: Care, Health & Development, 33*(3), 275–281.

Chak, K., & Leung, L. (2004). Shyness and locus of control as predictors of Internet addiction and Internet use. *CyberPsychology & Behavior, 7*(5), 559–570.

Cheuk, W. S., & Chan, Z. C. Y. (2007). ICQ (I Seek You) and adolescents: A quantitative study in Hong Kong. *CyberPsychology & Behavior, 10*(1), 108–114.

Cheung, L. M., & Wong, W. S. (2011). The effects of insomnia and Internet addiction on depression in Hong Kong adolescents: An exploratory cross-sectional analysis. *Journal of Sleep Research, 20*(2), 311–317.

China Youth Internet Association (CYIA). (2010). *China youth Internet addiction report*. Retrieved May 16, 2011, from http://mat1.gtimg.com/edu/pdf/wangyinbaogao.pdf

CNNIC. (2010). *2009 research report of China youth Internet behaviors*. Retrieved September 18, 2010, from http://www.cnnic.net.cn/html/Dir/2010/04/23/5814.htm

CNNIC. (2011). *The 27th statistical survey report on Internet development in China*. Retrieved April20,2011,fromhttp://www.cnnic.net.cn/dtygg/dtgg/201101/P020110119328960192287.pdf

Correa, T., Hinsley, A. W., & de Zuniga, H. G. (2010). Who interacts on the web?: The intersection of users' personality and social media use. *Computers in Human Behavior, 26*, 247–253.

Ellison, N., Lampe, C., Steinfield, C., & Vitak, J. (2010). With a little help from my friends: How social network sites affect social capital processes. In Z. Papacharissi (Ed.), *The networked self: Identity, community, and culture on social network sites* (pp. 124–146). New York: Routledge.

Fallows, D. (2007). *Internet addiction in China*. Retrieved May 15, 2011, from http://www.pewinternet.org/Commentary/2007/September/Internet-Addiction-in-China.aspx

Geng, Y., Su, L., & Cao, F. (2006). A research on emotion and personality characteristics in junior 1 high school students with Internet addiction disorders. *Chinese Journal of Clinical Psychology, 14*, 153–155.

Ghassemzadeh, L., Shahraray, M., & Moradi, A. (2008). Prevalence of Internet addiction and comparison of Internet addicts and non-addicts in Iranian high schools. *CyberPsychology & Behavior, 11*(6), 731–733.

Gibbs, J., Ellison, N., & Heino, R. (2006). Self-presentation in online personals: The role of anticipated future interaction, self-disclosure, and perceived success in Internet dating. *Communication Research, 33*, 152–180.

Gong, J., Chen, X., Zeng, J., Li, F., Zhou, D., & Wang, Z. (2009). Adolescent addictive Internet use and drug abuse in Wuhan, China. *Addiction Research & Theory, 17*(3), 291–305.

Gu, W. (2007, July 8). Six middle school students were stuck in the Internet. *Workers Daily*, B08.

Huang, H., & Leung, L. (2009). Instant messaging addiction among teenagers in China: Shyness, alienation, and academic performance decrement. *CyberPsychology & Behavior, 12*(6), 675–679.

Katz, E., Blumler, J. G., & Gurevitch, M. (1974). Utilization of mass communication by the individual. In J. D. Blumler & E. Katz (Eds.), *The uses of mass communications: Current perspectives on gratifications research* (pp. 19–32). Beverly Hills: Sage.

Ko, C. H., Yen, J. Y., Yen, C. F., Lin, H. C., & Yang, M. J. (2007). Factors predictive for incidence and remission of Internet addiction in young adolescents: A prospective study. *CyberPsychology & Behavior, 10*(4), 545–551.

Ko, C. H., Yen, J. Y., Yen, C. F., Chen, C. S., Weng, C. C., & Chen, C. C. (2008). The association between Internet addiction and problematic alcohol use in adolescents: The problem behavior model. *CyberPsychology & Behavior, 11*(5), 571–576.

Kramer, N. C., & Winter, S. (2008). Impression management 2.0. The relationship of self-esteem, extraversion, self-efficacy, and self-presentation within social network sites. *Journal of Media Psychology, 20*(3), 106–116.

Lam, L., Peng, Z., Mai, J., & Jing, J. (2009). Factors associated with Internet addiction among adolescents. *CyberPsychology & Behavior, 12*(5), 551–555.

Leary, M. R. (1996). *Self-presentation: Impression management and interpersonal behavior*. Boulder: Westview Press.

Leung, L. (2008). Leisure boredom, sensation seeking, self-esteem, addiction symptoms and patterns of mobile phone use. In E. Korini, S. Utz, M. Tanis, & S. B. Barnes (Eds.), *Mediated interpersonal communication*. New York: Routledge.

Li, X., Li, Z., & Xie, W. (2006). Epidemiological investigation on Internet addiction among middle school students in Hefei. *Chinese Mental Health Journal, 20*, 51–54.

Lin, C., Lin, S., & Wu, C. (2009). The effects of parental monitoring and leisure boredom on adolescents' Internet addiction. *Adolescence, 44*(176), 993–1004.

Liu, Y. (2007). Psycho-social related factors of junior high school students with Internet addiction disorder. *Chinese Journal of Clinical Psychology, 15*, 422–423.

Liu, Y., & Ma, L. (2011). *Failing to meet netfriend, 17-year old boy committed suicide in Zhangjiakou*. Retrieved July 7, 2011, from http://yanzhao.yzdsb.com.cn/system/2011/04/21/011070522.shtml

Nalwa, K., & Anand, A. P. (2003). Internet addiction in students: A cause of concern. *CyberPsychology & Behavior, 6*(6), 653–656.

Odaci, H., & Kalkan, M. (2010). Problematic Internet use, loneliness and dating anxiety among young adult university students. *Computers & Education, 55*(3), 1091–1097.

Tsai, C. C., & Lin, S. J. (2003). Internet addiction of adolescents in Taiwan: An interview study. *CyberPsychology & Behavior, 6*, 649–652.

Xinhua News Agency. (2006). *Parents sue online game seller for son's suicide.* Retrieved July 7, 2011, from http://www.china.org.cn/english/China/16811.htm

Yang, S. C., & Tung, C. J. (2007). Comparison of Internet addicts and non-addicts in Taiwanese high school. *Computer in Human Behavior, 23*(1), 79–96.

Yang, S., Huang, Y., & Cong, F. (2002, April 24). Six days and nights adolescent lost in the Internet. *Xinhua Daily Telegraph,* 006.

Yuen, C. N., & Lavin, M. J. (2004). Internet dependence in the collegiate population: The role of shyness. *CyberPsychology & Behavior, 7*(4), 379–383.

Zhuang, R., & Ai, D. (2010, November 30). The impact of QQ happy farm on Adolescents. *Hangzhou Daily,* B04.

Chapter 2
Literature Review

This chapter reviews the previous literature related to this study. It discusses the major findings concerning the following topics: definitions of social media; current social media penetration in China; U&G studies—both history and the most recent findings in U&G studies on IM, SNS, blogs, and microblogs; Internet addiction—both in Greater China and western countries; the sociopsychological traits of the need for affiliation, impression management, narcissism and leisure boredom, and the relationship of these traits with Internet use, social media use, and Internet addiction; and positive or negative impact of Internet use, social media use, and Internet addiction on adolescents' academic performance and social capital. Grounded in previous literature, hypotheses are proposed and research questions are raised.

2.1 What Are Social Media?

Social media are applications that enable people to interact with each other and build social networks that increase social capital (Barnes 2008). This massive phenomenon is changing the way we create and use content (Comm 2010). As Comm (2010) suggested, the definition of social media is vague. In the broadest sense, it describes a form of publishing in which stories are exchanged rather than published within a community "like a chat in a restaurant" (Comm 2010, p. 3). In the narrowest sense, however, social media describes how publishers can distribute their messages to thousands of people, encouraging them to build strong connections and firm loyalty (Comm 2010).

Castells (2000) describes the network society as a culture that is constructed virtually "by pervasive, interconnected, and diversified media systems" (p. 1). In addition, the network society is based on the idea of using computer-mediated communication (CMC) to promote cooperation between two or more individuals and build social capital (Barnes 2008). Comm (2010) suggested that perhaps the best definition of social media is that its content has been created by its audience because the "social" part of social media means that "publishing is now about participation"

H. Huang, *Social Media Generation in Urban China: A Study of Social Media Use and Addiction among Adolescents*, Understanding China,
DOI 10.1007/978-3-642-45441-7_2, © Springer-Verlag Berlin Heidelberg 2014

(Comm 2010, p. 3). Those who use social media sufficiently create not only content but also conversations, and those conversations combine further to create communities (Comm 2010). Spannerworks (2007) gave a similar working definition of social media as new kinds of online media that share most or all of the characteristics of participation, openness, conversation, community, and connectedness. Kaplan and Haenlein (2010) defined social media more theoretically as "a group of Internet-based applications that build on the ideological and technological foundations of Web 2.0, which allow the creation and exchange of user-generated content" (p. 64).

The concept of "social media" might be new, but the idea of using media environments for socializing practices goes back to the age of the telegraph and telephone (Barnes 2008). Nowadays, popular social media include instant messenger (IM), social network sites (SNS), blogs, microblogs like Twitter, bulletin board systems (BBS), YouTube, and Wikipedia, for example.

Results from focus groups among adolescents in urban China indicated that in 2010, IM, SNS, blogs, and microblogs were their four most widely used social media. These results were in accord with the statistics reported by CNNIC (2010) showing that by the end of 2009, IM, blogs, and SNS were the three most popular online communication applications among adolescents in China. Microblog is added to the list because in the focus groups, adolescents pointed out that although microblog was a new kind of social medium, it had gained popularity quickly among them. One reason was that they could use microblogs through their mobile phones while they were at school during the day, although they had to do so "secretly." In their latest report, CNNIC also emphasized that microblogs were becoming more and more popular; by the end of 2010, 63 million microblogs users already existed, and an even greater number was predicted for 2011 (CNNIC 2011). For the reasons discussed above, the social media this study focuses on consist of IM, SNS, blogs, and microblogs.

2.2 Social Media and Their Penetration in China

2.2.1 Instant Messaging (IM)

IM is a computer application that allows synchronous text communication between two or more people through the Internet. Parties at both ends of a conversation see each line of text right after it is typed (line by line). Thus, IM is more like a written telephone conversation than an exchange of letters (Bambooweb Dictionary 2008). IM is a composite of e-mail, chat rooms, pagers, telephones, voice mail, caller ID, and bulletin boards with a multiparty "chat" model (Chung and Nam 2007). As a relational maintenance tool, IM has been used for entertainment, work, and team relationships (Ramirez and Broneck 2003). In addition, IM has been found useful when discussing topics that are uncomfortable to talk about in face-to-face situations (Lenhart et al. 2001). The IM discussed here includes QQ, MSN Messenger, Yahoo! Messenger, Skype, and all other kinds of IM applications.

According to CNNIC (2011), IM had 353 million users by the end of 2010, making it the most popular online communication application in China. Meanwhile, IM is also the most popular mobile phone online application (CNNIC 2011). The number of IM users is still increasing every year, with an increase of 29.5 % more users in 2010 compared with 2009. More than three-quarters (77.1 %) of Internet users in China use IM (CNNIC 2011), while more than four out of five (80.5 %) middle-school Internet users use IM (CNNIC 2010). These statistics indicate the dominant popularity of IM in China, particularly among middle-school adolescents.

2.2.2 Social Network Sites (SNS)

SNS are "web-based services that allow individuals to (1) construct a public or semi-public profile within a bounded system, (2) articulate a list of other users with whom they share a connection, and (3) view and traverse their list of connections and those made by others within the system" (Boyd and Ellison 2007, p. 211). SNS enable users to connect with each other by creating personal information profiles, inviting friends to have access to those profiles, and sending messages and comments back and forth to each other (Kaplan and Haenlein 2010).

From another point of view, SNS are virtual collections of users' profiles (Raacke and Bonds-Raacke 2008). Those personal profiles can include any type of information, such as text description, photos, audio, or video (Kaplan and Haenlein 2010). The profiles can be shared with others to create lists of companions and maintain contact with them (Raacke and Bonds-Raacke 2008). The lists show each user's network, that is, the user's profile or updated messages are accessible by individuals included on the user's list (Lenhart 2009). SNS allow a varying amount of flexibility in communication style (Murphy 2005).

SNS have become popular among Chinese netizens in the past 2 years, especially since the dominant 2009 popularity of the SNS game, "Happy Farm." SNS had 235 million users in China by the end of 2010. The number is still expanding, with an increase of 33.7 % in 2010 compared with 2009 (CNNIC 2011). SNS have garnered 51.4 % participation among Chinese Internet users (CNNIC 2011), while 40.1 % of the middle-school Internet users participate in them (CNNIC 2010). Renren (previously known as Xiaonei) and Kaixin are the two most widely used SNS among Chinese users.

The SNS discussed in this study include Renren, Kaixin, Facebook (which has very few Chinese users because of the Great Firewall of China), and all other kinds of social networking websites.

2.2.3 Blogs

Blogs are special types of websites that usually display date-stamped entries in reverse chronological order (OECD 2007). On these sites, blog owners can share their feelings, photos, ideas, issues, and opinions (Huang et al. 2008; Riva 2002). Blog users can also "develop an individualized web presence that reflects facets of their personal style and idiosyncratic intellectual approaches" (Oravec 2002, p. 622). A blog is like an online diary, one that usually is managed by only one person, but that provides the opportunity for blog readers to interact with the owner by adding comments (Kaplan and Haenlein 2010). Bloggers can select personally contextualized information, present individual viewpoints, and invite critical comments without any pressure from external agendas (Blood 2002). Anyone can publish on the site, and their voices can be heard, communicated, and connected (Jung et al. 2007).

Blog is now the second most popular online communication application in China, with 295 million users by the end of 2010 (CNNIC 2011). The number of bloggers is greater every year, with an increase of 33 % in 2010 compared with 2009. Approximately 64.4 % of the Internet users in China use blogs (CNNIC 2011), while 69.5 % of middle-school Internet users use blogs (CNNIC 2010). CNNIC (2011) suggested that the rapid growth of blog use is related closely to the rapid growth of IM and SNS use. One major reason is that many IM and SNS applications now provide personal blog spaces. Thus, blogs based on the interpersonal networks built on IM and SNS are now important media for deeper communication and mutual understanding among friends and acquaintances.

2.2.4 Microblogs

The microblog can be considered a "mini blog." It is an online platform where users post short messages of up to 140 characters and share with others within their social networks (Murphy 2008) comments about what they are doing, reading, or watching online or any other topic (Martinez 2009). People use microblogs to describe their current status and daily activities in short posts and to seek or share information (Java et al. 2007). Anyone with an Internet connection or a mobile phone can use microblogs through text messaging or web browsers (Johnson and Yang 2009). In microblogs, users can subscribe to one's feed and become that person's "follower" (Honeycutt and Herring 2009). On a microblog interface, an individual user can see the messages published by those he or she follows, while his or her published messages can be seen by his or her followers.

Microblogs grew rapidly in China during 2010, becoming popular not only among Internet users but also among mobile phone users. By the end of 2010, microblog users had reached 63 million in China. There are 13.8 % of the Internet users use microblogs, while 15.5 % of the mobile phone Internet users use microblogs (CNNIC 2011). Microblogs are now becoming important social media for self-expression, interpersonal communication, information seeking, and social sharing.

Although the above statistics showed the general popularity of social media among Chinese Internet users, particularly among adolescents, they did not indicate in detail the degree of use for each kind of social medium in terms of the time or number of friends. As this study focuses on social media addiction among adolescents in urban Chinese cities, it is first asked:

RQ_1: To what degree do adolescents in urban China use social media, including IM, SNS, blogs, and microblogs?

2.3 Uses and Gratifications

2.3.1 History

U&G is a psychological communication theory that focuses on studying how people use media. It attempts to explain how individuals use mass media to gratify their needs. U&G seeks to discover the underlying motives for an individual's use of the media and to identify the positive and negative consequences of individual media use (Katz et al. 1974). The principal elements of U&G research are the individual's social and psychological needs and motives to communicate, their communication behavior, and the consequences of such behavior (Rubin 2002). Katz et al. (1974) described the U&G approach to media studies as:

> (1) the social and psychological origins of (2) needs, which generate (3) expectations of (4) the mass media and other sources, which lead to (5) differential patterns of media exposure, resulting in (6) need gratifications and (7) other consequences, perhaps mostly unintended ones. (p. 20)

Research using the U&G approach has offered insights into the reasons why individuals use a certain medium, the socio-demographic or psychological differences among various types of media users, media behavior, and the relationship between gratifications-sought and gratifications-obtained resulting from motivations of media use (Papacharissi and Rubin 2000).

U&G uses a limited-effects media perspective, emphasizing that media effects are constrained by individual differences among users. It is based on certain assumptions (Katz et al. 1974):

(a) Individuals select media and media content actively rather than passively to satisfy their needs.
(b) Individuals use the media to fulfill certain expectations.
(c) Individuals' use of media can be conceived as goal oriented, and all kinds of media compete with each other to satisfy users.
(d) Individuals are aware of and can state their own motives for using media.
(e) Motives and gratifications of using media should be fully understood before addressing the cultural significance of media content to individuals.

Adolescent users of social media are considered to select actively the types of social media to fulfill their various needs for interpersonal communication channels. Social media compete with other computer-mediated communication (CMC) applications or other communication tools, such as mobile phones or telephones, to satisfy adolescents. Adolescents are aware of and can state their own motives for using social media.

One limitation of U&G assumptions is that they emphasize more on personal expectations. As social media are mainly for social purposes, it is possible for individuals to use social media for fulfilling social expectations as well.

Historically, the U&G approach has a long tradition in research concerning media uses and effects (Blumler and Katz 1974). According to Ruggiero (2000), Wimmer and Dominick (1994) suggested that U&G originated as early as the 1940s, when researchers began to pay attention to why people use a certain medium, while Dozier and Rice (1984) referred to the immediate-and-delayed-reward model of media gratification by Schramm (1949) as the starting point of U&G research. Early U&G research focused around the findings of Lasswell (1948) on why people use media. Lasswell (1948) identified three functions of mass communication: surveillance of the environment, correlation of events in the environment, and transmission of social heritage. Later, Wright (1960) completed the list by adding entertainment as the fourth function.

Early U&G research concentrated primarily on describing and classifying individual media uses and motives into a typology (Ruggiero 2000). For example, some U&G research studied newspaper reading (Berelson 1949), comics reading (Wolfe and Fiske 1949), and radio listening (Cantril and Allport 1935; Herzog 1944). However, these earlier studies neglected the relationship between media gratification and the psychological or sociological origins of individual needs (Ruggiero 2000).

U&G research during the 1950s and 1960s began to identify social and psychological variables as antecedents of media gratifications (Wimmer and Dominick 1994). Researchers also began to focus on analyzing the consequences of use rather than simply to classify the use (Klapper 1963). Many functions of media use were identified during that period, such as companionship, changing mood, relief from loneliness or boredom, and escape (Katz and Foulkes 1962; Mendelsohn 1964).

Later in the 1970s, Rosengren (1974) tried to refine U&G theoretically. He pointed out that an individual's basic needs, personal characteristics, and the social environment interact with each other, resulting in perceived problems and potential solutions for that individual (for example, loneliness and listening to the radio). These problems and solutions constitute the motives for seeking gratifications, which can be obtained from media consumption or other activities (Ruggiero 2000). Palmgreen and Rayburn (1979) proposed to study simultaneously the gratifications sought and obtained from media use, while researchers later differentiated gratifications-sought and gratifications-obtained as two different concepts that require separate examination (McLeod et al. 1982).

In the 1980s, U&G researchers reevaluated the concept of "active audience" (Levy and Windahl 1984). At that point, U&G regarded audiences "to be variably—not universally—active." That is, all audience members are "not equally active at all times" (Rubin 2002, p. 534). During that period of time, TV played a major role in U&G research. After identifying relaxation, companionship, passing time, learning, excitement, and escape as six reasons why children and adolescents use TV (Rubin 1979), Rubin (1984) further identified two types of TV viewers: ritualized users, who are habitual, time-passing viewers and instrumental users, who are selective and goal-oriented, using media content primarily for information. Studies also looked at different types of TV programming, such as cable TV in general (Shaver 1983), or specific content types such as soap opera (Lemish 1985), and religious TV (Abelman 1987; Pettersson 1986).

Ball-Rokeach and Defleur first proposed the media dependency theory in the 1970s, and it was conceptually elaborated and empirically assessed in the 1980s. According to this theory, media influence is determined in the ecological conception of a dependency relationship. That relationship originates from individual (micro), and moves through interpersonal (meso) to social environment and media system (macro conditions), results in structural dependency relations (macro relationships) (Ball-Rokeach and Jung 2009). Rubin (2002) pointed out that an individual's dependency upon a medium may result from motives or strategies for obtaining gratifications and from restricted functional alternatives.

Social media provide gratifications that satisfy certain needs for adolescents. When those expected gratifications can be obtained largely during the process of using social media, and functional alternatives available to the user are limited, it might result in dependency.

As information and communication technologies (ICT) developed rapidly in the 1990s, new media technology brought many more media choices. Researchers have had more opportunities to apply the U&G approach to studying a wider range of popular media technology such as cable TV (Donohew et al. 1987; Jacobs 1995; LaRose and Atkin 1991), video cassette recorders (VCR) (Lin 1993), bulletin board systems (BBS) (James et al. 1995), computer and video games (Funk and Buchman 1996), and home computers (Perse and Dunn 1998).

At the beginning of the twenty-first century, the development of new technologies shifted focus from mass media to mediated interpersonal communication technology. The Internet and many mediated interpersonal communication devices have become very popular. As a result, a large number of U&G studies have been conducted on these new technologies, such as Internet use (Charney and Greenberg 2002; Leung 2003; Papacharissi and Rubin 2000; Stafford and Stafford 2004), Web use (Eighmey and McCord 1998; Ferguson and Perse 2000; Perse and Ferguson 2000), e-mail (Dimmick et al. 2000), BBS (Rafaeli 1986), Short Message Service (SMS) (Leung 2007), mobile phone (Auter 2007; Leung and Wei 2000; Wei and Lo 2006), and personal digital assistant (PDA) (Peters and Allouch 2005). There have also been many U&G studies about social media such as IM, SNS, blogs, and microblogs in recent years. The following section will discuss the latest U&G studies on social media.

2.3.2 U&G Studies on IM

As the most popular online communication tool, IM has attracted the attention of many researchers. Many of these studies have investigated IM use from a U&G approach.

As early as 10 years ago, Leung (2001) investigated college students' motives for chatting on ICQ and found that for college students, relaxation, entertainment, and fashion are instrumental motives for using ICQ, while inclusion, affection, sociability, and escape are their intrinsic motives. Students who use ICQ heavily are motivated by affection and sociability (Leung 2002). Ljungstrand and Segerstad (2000) suggested that college students use IM both to collaborate on assignments and to coordinate social activities. Recchiuti (2003) compared the use of IM with e-mail and an online chat room and found that students used IM more than the other two for social and ritualized communication, which provided the unique gratifications of companionship and anonymity for users.

Cheuk and Chan (2007) studied high school students in Hong Kong and suggested that the main reasons for their use of ICQ were entertainment, relaxation, and socializing. Huang (2008) also studied IM use among Chinese adolescents and found that a sense of belonging, peer influence, escape, avoiding presence, and habit as gratifications. Ramirez et al. (2008) compared the gratification niches of IM with e-mail and telephone and found that among 23 general gratifications statements, IM had a substantial niche overlap with e-mail and the cell phone, which indicated a certain degree of substitutability between these media.

Hwang (2009) discussed both gratifications-sought and gratifications-obtained from IM use among college students in the United States. He found that college students used IM to seek five gratifications: interpersonal utility, social utility, convenience, entertainment/relaxation, and information needs. Convenience and social utility were two of the most salient for both gratifications-sought and gratifications-obtained. Quan-Haase and Young (2010) compared Facebook and IM use from a U&G perspective and found that Facebook is about having fun and knowing about the social activities in one's social network, while IM is more suitable for maintaining and developing relationships.

2.3.3 U&G Studies on SNS

Since SNS has become very popular these days, many recent U&G studies have examined this form of social media.

Raacke and Bonds-Raacke (2008) studied SNS among students at a university in the United States. They found that popular gratifications-obtained from having a MySpace or Facebook account included keeping in touch with old and current friends, sharing photos, and making new friends as well as locating old friends. Some less commonly reported gratifications included learning about events, feeling connected, sharing information about oneself, satisfying academic purposes, and dating.

Park and his colleagues (2009) surveyed 1,715 university students about their Facebook use and found that socializing, entertainment, information, and self-status seeking were the four major gratifications. The researchers pointed out that individuals who participate in Facebook to satisfy their socializing needs are generally interested in meeting and talking with others, as well as obtaining peer support and a sense of community. Users gain entertainment gratification by being involved in Facebook groups for their leisure and amusement needs. University students satisfy their information needs by learning about on- and off-campus events or details regarding specific products and services through Facebook. Users were also likely to participate in Facebook to gain and maintain their personal status by participating in online groups. These university students also pointed out that they joined Facebook groups because they felt peer pressure to do so, wanted to make themselves look cool, and to develop their career (Park et al. 2009). After both surveying and interviewing undergraduate students, Quan-Haase and Young (2010) added to the SNS gratifications list that using SNS is a way to pass time, gain or give affection, keep up with fashion, and share problems.

Cheung et al. (2011) recently proposed an interesting idea of what users express by "we-intention" when they use SNS. They pointed out that "we-intention" emphasizes that it is the presence of "we," that is, together as a group instead of each individually, that creates an intention to continue using SNS, and "this is a joint intention made by a group of people that everyone will perform his own part to perform a joint action together with others" (p. 1338).

Using qualitative research, Dunne and Lawlor (2010) studied the gratifications from SNS and found that the SNS use among young people (aged 12–14) was motivated by communicating, making friends, identity creation and management, entertainment, escapism and alleviation of boredom, information search, and interacting with boys. Meanwhile, the gratifications-obtained from using SNS were quite different. They included portraying one's ideal image, peer acceptance, relationship maintenance, and safety from embarrassment and rejection (Dunne and Lawlor 2010). Urista and her colleagues (2009) held focus groups to examine the use of MySpace and Facebook among young adults. They identified five gratifications as efficient communication, convenient communication, curiosity about others, popularity, and relationship formation and reinforcement.

2.3.4 U&G Studies on Blogs

Jung et al. (2007) found that entertainment, self-expression, professional advancement, passing time, communication with family and friends, and following the trend are key motives for blogging. Lee et al. (2008) proposed similar motives, including self-presentation, relationship management, keeping up with trends, information sharing, information storage, and entertainment.

Leung (2009) studied gratifications of user-generated content on the Internet, such as blogs, Wikipedia, and YouTube and found the following gratifications-sought (1) recognition need, illustrating that Internet users try to establish their personal identity, gain respect and confidence, and demonstrate their expertise through generating online content; (2) cognitive needs, stating that users try to broaden their knowledge base, keep abreast with the latest developments, and know what is happening in the community through online contents; (3) social needs, reflecting how Internet users find the Internet a comfortable place to reveal their feelings, share views and experiences, and update their latest information to family and friends; and (4) entertainment needs, indicating that generating content online cannot only pass the time but also be entertaining, fun, interesting, and trendy.

In a content analysis of 358 randomly selected blogs in the Polish language, Trammel et al. (2004) identified six major motivations for blogging: self-expression, social interaction, entertainment, passing the time, gaining information, and professional advancement.

In analyzing users' gratifications or motives for reading and browsing blogs, Wang and Fesenmaier (2004) suggested that people who participate in blogging activities are mainly for the social benefits—they hope to provide assistance or discuss their views with other members. Huang et al. (2008) revealed that the motives for reading blogs were affective exchanges, information search, entertainment, and getting on the bandwagon. The authors illustrated the effects of these motives on three major responses: interaction intentions, opinion acceptance, and word-of-mouth intentions. They pointed out that readers who focus on affective exchanges believe what they read in blog messages and interact with bloggers. For those motivated by information search and entertainment motives, blogging is mainly aimed at opinion acceptance; they also view blogs as trustworthy sources and transmit messages to others.

2.3.5 U&G Studies on Microblogs

Microblogs were introduced not very long ago and recently have become more and more popular. Microblogs have begun to attract researchers' attention lately, and so far just a few researches have discussed this form of social media.

Martinez (2009) interviewed some microbloggers in Southeast Texas who wrote about their everyday happenings, made friends with similar interest through their microblog, and organized regular offline meetings. Those microbloggers pointed out that using microblog is for gratification of an immediate emotional response.

Johnson and Yang (2009) studied both the gratifications-sought and gratifications-obtained of using Twitter. They identified 15 gratifications-obtained variables: be entertained, have fun, relax, pass the time, keep in touch with friends or family, see what others are up to, express oneself freely, communicate more easily, communicate with many people at the same time, get information, learn interesting things, give or receive advice, participate in discussions, meet new people, and share information with others. The authors grouped these gratifications into social and information motives for using Twitter. Interestingly, their data suggested that Twitter is used primarily as an information source rather than for satisfying social needs.

In contrast, Chen (2011) found the most important gratification-sought from using Twitter is a need to connect with others, and the more months a person is active on Twitter and the more hours per week the person spends on Twitter, the more gratifications he or she obtains. U&G research on microblogging is scarce and further investigation is needed.

The literature review of U&G research shows that for over 70 years the U&G perspective has developed into a more sophisticated theoretical model. The inquiry has shifted from a mechanistic perspective focusing on the direct effects of media on users to a psychological perspective stressing individual use and choice (Rubin 2002; Ruggiero 2000). Lin (1996) stressed the importance and strength of U&G theory in investigating "mediated communication situations via a single or multiple sets of psychological needs, psychological motives, communication channels, communication contents, and psychological gratifications within a particular cultural context" (p. 574).

For these reasons, U&G approach is adopted in this research to study social media use and addiction. Thus, this study asks and hypothesizes:

RQ_2: What gratifications do adolescents in urban China obtain from using social media?

H_1: The more the adolescents in urban China find social media gratifying, the more they will use social media.

According to William Miller (2006), addiction is fundamentally a problem of motivation. For example, shopping addicts were motivated mainly by escape (Elliott et al. 1996). Only a few studies discuss the relationship between gratifications and media addiction. Rubin (1984) suggested that, compared with instrumental use of media, ritualistic/habitual use of media was more likely to relate to media dependency. Supporting Rubin's proposition, Park (2005) found that ritualistic motives explained mobile phone addiction more strongly than instrumental motives. TV addicts watched television mainly to divert their disturbing thoughts and to pass the time (McIlwraith 1998). Internet gratifications such as diversion, virtual community, and relationship maintenance were likely to lead to Internet addiction, while information seeking and aesthetic experience negatively explained Internet addiction (Song et al. 2004). Internet addicts mainly used the Internet to seek social support, but seldom used it to seek information (Tao et al. 2007). To understand further the relationships between gratifications and media addiction, this study applied U&G approach to investigate the relationships between social media gratifications and social media addiction. The next section reviews the literature of Internet and social media addiction.

2.4 Internet Addiction and Social Media Addiction

2.4.1 Internet Addiction

Traditionally, the concept of "addiction" was based on a medical model and properly reserved for bodily and psychological dependence on a physical substance. Researchers have argued that the concept of addiction should be widened to cover a broader range of behaviors (Lemon 2002; Orford 2001; Shaffer 1996). Peele (1985) suggested that any compulsive or overused activity could be considered as addiction.

Griffiths (1996) proposed the concept of "technological addiction," which is nonchemical but behavioral in nature and involves excessive human-machine interaction. Technological addiction can be either passive, such as viewing television, or active, such as gaming on the computer or chatting online and usually comprises inducing and reinforcing features that may contribute to the promotion of addictive tendencies (Griffiths 1996). It also features the core components of addiction, including salience, mood modification, tolerance, withdrawal, conflict, and relapse (Griffiths 1998). Griffiths (1998) argued that any behavior that fulfills these criteria could be defined operationally as addiction. Some research also supported the notion that excessive use of technology can be considered problematic (Griffiths and Hunt 1998; Shotton 1989).

Internet addiction disorder (IAD) was first proposed by Ivan Goldberg in 1995. Derived from the substance-dependence criteria of the *Diagnostic and Statistical Manual of Mental Disorders* (4th Ed.) (DSM-IV) (American Psychiatric Association 1994), IAD is the first listed Internet-related disorder. It is defined as a behavioral addiction consisting of six core components: salience, mood modification, tolerance, withdrawal symptoms, conflict, and relapse (Griffiths 1998). Young (1998) proposed that by using pathological gambling as a model, Internet addiction could be defined as an impulse-control disorder that does not involve an intoxicant. Young (1996) characterized Internet addiction as staying online for pleasure averaging 38 h or more per week, largely in chat rooms, and concluded that Internet addiction can shatter families, relationships, and careers.

Utilizing an adapted version of the criteria for pathological gambling defined by the DSM-IV, Young (1998) developed eight criteria to provide a screening instrument for addictive Internet use. Individuals who meet five of eight criteria for Internet addiction qualify as addicts: (1) preoccupation with Internet use; (2) need for longer amount of time online; (3) repeated attempts to reduce Internet use; (4) mood modification on Internet use; (5) staying online longer than intended; (6) loss of significant relationship, job, and educational or career opportunity; (7) deception around time spent online; and (8) Internet use as a way of escaping from problems. Several other studies on Internet addiction were conducted over the past decade (Beard 2002; Beard and Wolf 2001; Chak and Leung 2004; Griffiths 2000; Leung 2004; Scherer 1997; Young 1999).

2.4.2 Internet Addiction Among Adolescents

Both researchers and the Chinese government have paid a great deal of attention to Internet addiction problems among adolescents in recent years. Besides the official reports mentioned in the introduction section of this study, many other scholars also focused their studies on Internet addiction among adolescents in China.

Cao and Su (2007) surveyed 2,620 Chinese high school students in Changsha and found that 2.4 % of the respondents were addicted to the Internet. Those adolescents who were addicted to the Internet showed significantly lower time-management skills than the normal group in the sense of control over time, value of time, and time efficacy. Internet-addicted adolescents also showed significantly more emotional symptoms, conduct problems, hyperactivity, and less pro-social behaviors than the normal group.

In Guangzhou, among 1,560 high school students, 10.2 % were found moderately addicted to the Internet, 0.6 % were severely addicted, and boys were more likely to be addicted than girls. The study also found drinking behavior, family dissatisfaction, and experience of recent stressful events were all associated with Internet addiction among adolescents (Lam et al. 2009).

In another big Chinese city, Wuhan, Gong, and his colleagues (2009) found among 3,018 adolescents, 5 % were addicted to the Internet, and the adolescents' use of drugs and the intention to use drugs were significantly related to Internet addiction. Other studies also used Young's 8-item or 20-item scale to study adolescents' Internet addiction and found Internet addiction levels among adolescents ranging from 3.5 to 11.34 % (Geng et al. 2006; Li et al. 2006; Liu 2007).

Many studies have focused on adolescent Internet addiction in Greater China, including Hong Kong and Taiwan. As early as 2004, Chak and Leung (2004) surveyed among the net generation in Hong Kong, most of whom were adolescents. Results showed that 14.7 % of them were Internet addicts, and the shyer the person was, the more likely she or he was addicted to Internet. The study also indicated that adolescents who were addicted to the Internet made intense and frequent use of it, with more days per week and longer time each session, especially for online interpersonal communication via ICQ and chat room. A recent study among 719 Hong Kong adolescents found that 17.2 % were addicted to the Internet and that Internet addiction was significantly correlated with the adolescents' depression and insomnia (Cheung and Wong 2011).

Yang and Tung (2007) studied 1,708 Taiwan high school students and identified 13.8 % as Internet addicts. The results showed that on average, the Internet addicts spent almost twice as many hours online as the nonaddicts and that surfing with social and entertainment motivations were positively associated with Internet addiction. It is interesting that Internet-addicted adolescents perceived the Internet to have significantly more negative influences on daily routines than nonaddicts, such as school performance and teacher and parental relations. However, both Internet addicts and nonaddicts adolescents considered that Internet use could enhance their peer relations.

A survey conducted by Ko and his colleagues (2008) among 2,114 high school students in Taiwan showed that Internet addiction was associated with problematic alcohol use. Ko and his colleagues (2007) also did a longitudinal study in Taiwan on Internet addiction among 517 young adolescents from junior middle school over a 1-year follow-up. The results revealed that within 1 year, 7.5 % of the nonaddicts became addicts, while 49.5 % of the addicts went into remission. They found that low self-esteem, low family function, and more online game playing predicted the Internet addiction, while low hostility and low interpersonal sensitivity predicted remission of Internet addiction.

In an in-depth interview among ten Taiwanese adolescents who were Internet addicts, Tsai and Lin (2003) found that almost all the adolescents exhibited most of the symptoms of Internet addiction, including compulsive use, tolerance, withdrawal, and related problems of school, health, family, finance, and time management. The respondents stated that they were addicted to the messages and activity on the Internet, but not by the Internet as a medium per se because the Internet helped them to relieve their depression. The adolescents interviewed self-declared that they were Internet addicts, but commented they did not know what to do about the problem.

Internet addiction is a problem not only for adolescents in China; it also presents headaches for parents and teachers all over the world. In an online survey in Italy, Young's Internet Addiction Test was administered to groups of people who differed in terms of gender, age, and occupation (Ferraro et al. 2007). Results revealed that adolescents were more at risk than adults for Internet addiction, "perceiving a compromised social and individual quality of their life that led them to make a compensatory usage of the Internet" (p. 174). Furthermore, nightly users were more at risk for developing an Internet addiction disorder because it diminished their quality of life and disabled their time control (Ferraro et al. 2007).

In Greece, Siomos and his colleagues (2008) surveyed 2,200 Greek adolescent students and showed that 8.2 % of them were addicted to the Internet, mainly male students who play online games and visit Internet cafés. In Iran, a study conducted in Iranian high schools revealed that, among 1,968 high school students, 977 students were Internet users: 37 were classified as Internet addicts, 304 as possible Internet addicts, and 636 as moderate users. Researchers found that Internet addicts were lonelier than moderate users and had lower self-esteem and poorer social skills (Ghassemzadeh et al. 2008).

Most of the above-mentioned research discussed Internet addiction as a general phenomenon. Griffiths (1998) proposed that Internet addiction could originate from one or more aspects of Internet use, including the process of typing, the medium of communication, and the lack of face-to-face contact, Internet contents, or online social activities. Other researchers also suggested that Internet addiction could further be categorized into online game addiction, cyber-sexual addiction, cyber-relationship addiction, online information addiction, and online shopping addiction and so on (Liang 2006; Tao et al. 2007). Although cyber-relationship addiction was mentioned, none of previous research has ever tested it empirically. To fill the gap, this study focuses on examining social media addiction.

2.4.3 *Social Media Addiction*

Social media such as IM, SNS, blogs, and microblogs are very popular these days. Adolescents spend a great deal of time on them, and some heavy users might be addicted.

Yuen and Lavin (2004) found that the length of time Internet dependents spent on IM was twice as much as that spent by nondependents, while Anderson (1999) found that daily use of synchronous communication Internet applications among Internet-dependent students was nearly 10 times as high as the use by nondependent students. Leung (2004) suggested that being emotionally open on the net and heavy use of ICQ were the most influential factors in predicting problematic use of the Internet among the net generation. This study reinforces research by Wellman (1996) who found that Internet dependents spent most of their time in the synchronous communication environment, engaging in interactive activities including ICQ for pleasure seeking or escape. Research by a nonprofit youth organization, Breakthrough (2000), showed that 5 % of the respondents who were secondary school students in Hong Kong were addicted to ICQ.

A study by Huang and Leung (2009) on IM addiction among adolescents in China found that 9.7 % of respondents were addicts. They found four addiction symptoms:

1. Preoccupation with IM, that is, acting annoyed when interrupted during an online chat, feeling preoccupied by online chatting and fantasizing about chatting online when offline, feeling depressed and moody when unable to chat online, sacrificing sleep to chat online, and needing to increase IM time to achieve satisfaction.
2. Loss of relationships due to overuse of IM revealed that addicted adolescents hide the length of time they spend chatting online, try to cut down their IM use but failing, choose to spend more time chatting online than going out with friends, and jeopardize friendships or educational opportunities because of online chatting.
3. Loss of control, illustrated by adolescents being unable to control the time they spend on IM; addicts always spend more time on IM than they intended, neglect other responsibilities and obligations, resulting in complaints from family and friends.
4. Escape, indicated that adolescents use IM as an alternative way to escape from responsibilities; they chat online when they are in a bad mood, and they always anticipate chatting online again.

Results of their study also showed that shyness and alienation from family, peers, and school are significantly and positively associated with the level of IM addiction among Chinese adolescents (Huang and Leung 2009).

In a case study, Karaiskos and his colleagues (2010) stated that a 24-year-old woman was referred to a clinic due to excessive use of SNS, which severely interfered with her daily life. She had been spending approximately 5 h per day checking her Facebook webpage and already accumulated over 400 web friends in the 8 months since she began to use Facebook. She ceased several of her routine activities, remained home most of the day in order to check her Facebook, and lost her job as a waitress because she repeatedly left her post to visit the nearest Internet café. During her examination at the clinic, she took out her mobile phone and tried to establish an Internet connection to check her Facebook account. Karaiskos and his colleagues (2010) concluded that Facebook addiction can be considered an "urge-driven disorder" with a strong compulsive component and suggested that Facebook addiction may be another distinct subcategory of Internet addiction.

In an article called "Blogs: My New Addiction," Bates reported that writing and reading blogs can also qualify as new addiction (2003). A study in Greece applying Young's addiction scale to 646 Greek college students showed that 7.9 % of them were addicted to the Internet, and that on average, those Internet-addicted students spent more time per week on blogs, chat rooms, and forums than nonaddicted students did (Frangos 2009).

USA Today organized an interesting activity in which it tried to put some of its readers with addiction to their virtual connections "on a digital diet." One of the participants stated that after she downloaded the Twitter and Facebook applications to her BlackBerry, "thumbing became an obsession," and she really needed a digital-free virtual vacation away from her virtual connections (Barker 2009). It seems that social media addiction really exists and is becoming pervasive worldwide.

According to the above literature review, the heavy users of social media tend to be gratified by them and are likely to be heavily immersed in social media for various online activities. To explore the latest situation of social media addiction in China, especially among urban Chinese adolescents, this study raised the following research questions and hypotheses:

RQ_3: To what degree are adolescents in urban China addicted to social media, and who are the social media addicts?

RQ_4: What symptoms of social media addiction can be identified among adolescents in urban China?

$H_{2.1}$: The more the adolescents in urban China use social media, the more likely they will be addicted to social media.

$H_{2.2}$: The more the adolescents in urban China find social media gratifying, the more likely they will be addicted to social media.

2.4.4 Parents' Role in Adolescents' Internet Addiction

Parents play an important role in dealing with the problems of Internet addiction among adolescents. In the China Youth Internet Addiction Report (CYIA 2010), the results showed that a higher percentage of adolescent Internet addicts than nonaddicts came from a less-educated or single-parent family or were not living with their parents. Internet-addicted adolescents tended to have less communication with their parents and enjoy less family harmony. It is worthy to note that Internet-addicted adolescents tended to come from families that imposed stricter discipline on them. The researchers explained that adolescents from these families might see the Internet as a haven to relieve pressure and escape from strict parental supervision, thus they could easily become addicts (CYIA 2010).

Some other studies also revealed that an authoritarian parenting style easily triggered rebellious behaviors and could result in counteraction (Tao et al. 2007; Zhao 2010). The study by the Addiction Medicine Center, General Hospital of Beijing Military Region showed that Internet-addicted adolescents consistently rated parental rearing behaviors as being over-intrusive, punitive, and lacking in responsiveness, suggesting that parenting and family functionality are important factors affecting adolescents' Internet addiction (Huang et al. 2010).

Huang and his colleagues (2009) found that lack of love from the family was associated significantly with Internet addiction. In another survey among 3,662 adolescents in Taiwan, results indicated that higher parent-adolescent conflict, habitual alcohol use by siblings, a perceived positive parental attitude toward adolescent substance use, and lower family function constructed a predictive model for adolescents' Internet addiction (Yen et al. 2007).

In contrast, participative and supportive parental monitoring can substantially decrease the probability of adolescents' becoming addicted to the Internet (Lin et al. 2009). Liu and Kuo (2007) also revealed from a group of Taiwanese students that healthy parent-child relationships and interpersonal relationships correlated negatively with Internet addiction.

Suggested by the above literature, it is hypothesized that:

$H_{2.3}$: The more strictly parents control the adolescents' online behavior, the more likely the adolescents will be addicted to social media.

2.5 Sociopsychological Traits

In previous addiction research, some studies suggested that it is the substance itself that causes addiction (Haddock and Beto 1988), some studies pointed out that certain genetic predispositions or brain differences might lead to addiction (Schuckit 1987), and some scholars believed that certain social and psychological traits might be related to addiction (Haddock and Beto 1988). This study discusses social media addiction from the standpoint of the effects of adolescents' sociopsychological traits.

2.5.1 Need for Affiliation

The need for affiliation is "the disposition to seek out or retain emotional relationships with people" (Veroff et al. 1984). The term describes an individual's desire to seek and maintain interpersonal relationships (Murray 1938). Seeking social dependency and belonging are common human behaviors (Bell and Daly 1984). The need for affiliation is the basis for human interaction; it is characterized by a strong tendency to seek connection and approval (Boyatzis 1973).

In this sense, Murray (1938) defined the need for affiliation as a tendency to receive social gratification from harmonious relationships and from a sense of communication with others. Since people exert large amounts of energy trying to obtain appreciation and affection from others (Bell and Daly 1984), the need for affiliation is a very important social motivation for human interaction. It can inspire more positive social interaction and the reciprocity of social relationships (Gable 2006).

People with a strong need for affiliation are more emotionally involved in relationships (Baron and Byrne 2003), and they show more concern in their thoughts and actions for achieving warm, close relationships with others (McClelland 1976). In the past, people with a strong need for affiliation wrote more letters (Lansing and Heyns 1959). In the Internet era, people, especially those with social limitations such as shyness and social anxiety, tend to be interested in using online communication to satisfy their need for affiliation (McKenna et al. 2002). CMC users with long-term interactions "have a greater affiliation need, seek and exchange more personal information, and evaluate each other more positively than those emerging from short-term interactions" (Walther et al. 2001, p. 112).

In online interpersonal interactions, the need for affiliation leads individual to establish and maintain self-image and to participate in various online activities, such as online chatting, online dating, and self-presentation (Gibbs et al. 2006). Research revealed that the greater an adolescent's need for affiliation, the more often they considered Internet communication to be deeper than face-to-face communication and the more interpersonal communication gratifications they would obtain from online communication (Peter and Valkenburg 2006).

Social media have a high potential to satisfy adolescents' need for affiliation. Chung and Nam (2007) suggested that the need for affiliation is an important variable for explaining why young people use IM because the frequency and the depth of a person's contacts with others depend on the degree to which he or she desires to maintain a positive and affective relationship with others. Chung and Nam (2007) also found in their research that IM users have significantly stronger need for affiliation than nonusers. Moreover, receiving friends' comments on personal blogs or microblogs indicate their care and attention, which may gladden and comfort those who have a strong need for affiliation.

In SNS, friends link to each other, write on each other's wall, and share many kinds of information. These makes adolescents feel like living in a close community and can satisfy their need for affiliation. Prior research also revealed that the need for affiliation is the main predictor for the intensity of SNS use (Zhou 2009). Social media can be ideal places for individuals to satisfy their need for affiliation and attract them to overly indulge in online interpersonal communication. Based on the literature, this study is designed to investigate the relationships among the need for affiliation, the gratifications, the level of using social media, and the social media addiction among adolescents.

Thus, it is hypothesized:

$H_{3.1}$: The stronger the need for affiliation of adolescents in urban China, the more they will find social media gratifying.

$H_{3.2}$: *The stronger the need for affiliation of adolescents in urban China, the more they will use social media.*

$H_{3.3}$: *The stronger the need for affiliation of adolescents in urban China, the more likely they will be addicted to social media.*

2.5.2 Impression Management

Goffman (1959) was among the first to acknowledge that individuals need to present themselves to others as an acceptable person. He described how the self-as-performer has a basic motivational core and how people can be strategic in managing the impression they give. Individuals wear masks, play roles, and present themselves in the ways they see themselves or in the ways they desire to be seen by others (Goffman 1959). They engage in complex intra-self negotiations in order to project a desired impression and maintain it through consistently performing coherent and complementary behaviors (Schlenker 1980; Schneider 1981).

Gilmore and his colleagues defined impression management as "conscious or unconscious attempts to influence images during interaction" (Gilmore et al. 1999, p. 322). Individuals manage their impressions when they wish to present a favorable image of themselves to others (Bolino et al. 2008). Thus, the concept of impression management is based on the assumption that individuals have an inherent need to be accepted and included and therefore act accordingly (Leary 1996). Self-presentation serves the goal of impression management (Goffman 1959). Therefore these two concepts are inseparable and interchangeable (Tedeschi and Riess 1981).

Jones and Pittman (1982) proposed that individuals typically use five impression management tactics: self-promotion, ingratiation, supplication, intimidation, and exemplification (Jones and Pittman 1982). The opportunity to manage impressions has been advanced by new communication technologies (Walther 1993). In the Internet era, people can make and remake themselves, choosing the details of their online impression (Mnookin 1996). Adolescents now can manage the impression they make through social media in many ways. These impression management opportunities come with the visual anonymity of the social media, providing users much greater degrees of freedom (Joinson 2003). People can manipulate various characteristics online to present themselves as more humorous, more friendly, or more likable than in daily life (Chester 2004). Dominick (1999) found that the five impression management tactics proposed by Jones and Pittman (1982) in offline communication extended to the online setting of personal home pages.

One feature that distinguishes online impression management from impression management in daily life lies in the full control users have over their published information, allowing the self-presentation to be more strategic (Kramer and Winter 2008). Online impression management can be based on longer and more systematic considerations than in a lively self-presentation (Leary 1996).

Thus, users can highlight certain aspects of themselves (Marwick 2005) or think about which photos convey the best images of themselves (Ellison et al. 2006). Studies showed that people tend to exaggerate and are not always honest when they present themselves online. For example, "fakesters" publish fake profile information in SNS and pretend to be more interesting and successful (Boyd 2004). Some individuals just switch between their "real" self and their "fake" self on SNS (Jung et al. 2007).

Thus, users actively participate in SNS to manage their impression (Kramer and Winter 2008). Indeed, social media provide an ideal place for impression management. In IM, users can manage their impression through chatting with others, trying to be more humorous, more interesting, or more knowledgeable. They can also provide an explanation to friends through IM if they did something wrong or deliver an apology if they hurt others. In SNS, users can manage their impression by creating personal profiles, uploading photos, writing on others' wall, or commenting on others' files. In blogs and microblogs, users can manage their impression through writing diaries, sharing their personal lives everywhere, or showing their care and friendliness to friends by commenting on others' blogs or microblogs.

Similar to Jones and Pittman (1982), Jung et al. (2007) discussed four impression management tactics in blogs: (1) demonstration of competence revealing that the bloggers showed their abilities, performance, and qualifications indirectly; (2) supplication indicating that the bloggers deprecated themselves indirectly and showed weakness to others; (3) exemplification showing that the bloggers tend to be self-disciplined and devoted to others; and (4) ingratiation demonstrating that the bloggers showed humor and familiarity in the blogs. Rosenberg (2009) also studied the management of online impressions and identified four self-presentation tactics used in Facebook: manipulation, damage control, self-promotion, and role model.

Many other features might also contribute to online impression management in social media. For example, more friends presented on one's profile leads to a positive evaluation; popularity and pleasantness were greater when profile owners had a larger number of linked friends (Kleck et al. 2007).

It is assumed that adolescents who excel at impression management will use social media more often for self-presentation and find social media more gratifying and efficient than face-to-face communications. If they are dedicated to managing their impression through social media instead of socializing with friends face to face in daily life, they are likely to be addicted to social media. Accordingly, the following research question and hypotheses are proposed:

RQ_5: What impression management tactics are used by urban Chinese adolescents for self-presentation in social media?

$H_{4.1}$: Adolescents in urban China who are better at impression management tactics tend to find social media more gratifying.

$H_{4.2}$: Adolescents in urban China who are better at impression management tactics tend to use social media more.

$H_{4.3}$: Adolescents in urban China who are better at impression management tactics are more likely to be addicted to social media.

2.5.3 Narcissism

Narcissism is a term derived the Greek myth about a handsome young man who falls in love with his own reflection in the water. In its extreme form, narcissism is a personality disorder that involves "grandiose views of self, an inflated sense of entitlement, and exploitative attitudes toward others" (American Psychiatric Association 1994). Most current research studied normal narcissism, which is a trait varying among people in the general population (Morf and Rhodewalt 2001).

Twenge and Campbell (2009) defined narcissism as excessive vanity and a sense of entitlement. People who show such qualities are more likely to lack empathy for others, behave aggressively when offended, and ignore the feelings of others. Miller (1981) proposed both core narcissism and narcissistic defenses. Core narcissism is the experience and expression of a very positive self-esteem, disproportionate to the individual's level of ability and achievement. This element of narcissism manifests as feelings of entitlement, grandiosity, and exhibitionism. In contrast, the narcissistic defenses appear to maintain the individual's level of self-esteem against threat (Miller 1985). However, narcissism should not be confused with self-esteem (Brown and Zeigler-Hill 2004).

Developmental psychology suggested that the grandiose and inflated self-views that characterize narcissism are part of normative self-development in young children. Young children typically are unable to differentiate their actual self-views from their ideal self-views (Harter 1999, 2006). Therefore, their self-views are unrealistically positive (Marsh et al. 1998). After children are about 7 or 8 years old, they start to base their self-views on social comparisons, making their self-views become more realistic. Thus, in growing children, self-views develop coexisting positive and negative attributes (Harter 1999, 2006).

Narcissism may emerge in response to either lack of parental attention and guidance (Kernberg 1975) or excessive parental admiration (Millon 1981). Narcissism increased significantly from age 14 to 18, followed by a slight but nonsignificant decline from ages 18 to 23 (Carlson and Gjerde 2009). Pinsky and Young (2009) suggested that a celebrity-obsessed culture is causing more narcissism in America.

Narcissism is reflected in SNS personal profiles or web pages, with more self-promoting contents (Correa et al. 2010), more frequent profile pictures and status updating, and choosing more attractive photos of themselves to affirm their inflated beliefs (Buffardi and Campbell 2008). Such narcissism can largely predict the intensity of SNS use (Correa et al. 2010). Narcissists are gratified largely by the exhibitionistic nature of SNS (Bibby 2008). If those narcissists enjoy the exhibitionistic nature of social media a great deal and overly indulge in self-presentation through social media, they will be most likely become social media addicts.

LaPorta (2009) discussed the unexpected consequences of heavy social media use such as MySpace, Facebook, YouTube, and Twitter, pointing out that heavy social media use would eliminate the real relationships and social contacts between people, prolong the normal narcissism of adolescence, and create isolation and alienation.

In a survey among 1,068 college students in 2009, Twenge and Campbell (2009) found that two-thirds of the students said that their current generation was more self-promoting, narcissistic, overconfident, and attention seeking than other generations. The authors also pointed out that such narcissistic traits revealed a very positive and inflated sense of self, which is illustrated by a preoccupation with MySpace, Facebook, and YouTube (Twenge and Campbell 2009).

The literature described above implies relationships among narcissism, gratifications, level of social media use, and social media addiction. Thus, it is hypothesized:

$H_{5.1}$: *Adolescents in urban China who are more narcissistic tend to find social media more gratifying.*

$H_{5.2}$: *Adolescents in urban China who are more narcissistic tend to use social media more.*

$H_{5.3}$: *Adolescents in urban China who are more narcissistic are more likely to be addicted to social media.*

2.5.4 Leisure Boredom

Boredom is regarded as a psychological or physiological condition (Mansikka 2009). It is a negative state of mind, reflecting an inner conflict between expected optimal and perceived actual experiences (Lin et al. 2009).

Having an abundance of time might lead to boredom in leisure time (Phillips 1993). Iso-Ahola and Weissinger (1990) looked specifically at the experience of boredom during leisure and suggested that a significant proportion of adolescents experience leisure time as unsatisfying mainly due to boredom. They defined leisure boredom as “the subjective perception that available leisure experiences are not sufficient to instrumentally satisfy needs for optimal arousal” (Iso-Ahola and Weissinger 1990, p. 4). Leisure boredom is likely a consequence of conflicting perceptions of having too much time available with too little to do (Hill and Perkins 1985).

Previous research showed that individuals who experience high levels of leisure boredom may engage in deviant activities such as substance abuse (Iso-Ahola and Crowley 1991). Youths who feel bored are more likely to engage in undesirable health behaviors such as smoking cigarettes and abusing alcohol (Caldwell and Smith 1995). Mattick and Baillie (1992) found that adolescent smokers cite relaxation and relief from boredom as reasons for smoking.

Ziervogel and his colleagues (1998) suggested that one of the most significant motives for the boys’ use of alcohol was that it alleviated boredom. They pointed out that boredom arose mainly from a lack of participation in other activities. Thus, some individuals need to find an enjoyable, time-consuming activity to indulge in (Ziervogel et al. 1998). Adolescents diagnosed with substance abuse or addiction according to the criteria of DSM-IV (American Psychiatric Association 1994) were more likely to experience leisure boredom than non-substance abusers (Iso-Ahola and Crowley 1991).

Avoiding boredom is a major motivation for Internet use (Lin and Yu 2008). Increasingly, social media allows adolescents, who otherwise have nothing to do, to engage in various activities online such as sharing photos or files, updating blogs, reading others' blogs or files, text chatting, or video chatting with friends. These activities probably occur most often during leisure time and in leisure settings.

A survey among Taiwanese adolescents indicated that leisure boredom largely increases the probability of Internet addiction, but family and outdoor activities, as well as participative and supportive parental monitoring, would decrease the probability of Internet addiction behavior (Lin et al. 2009). Leung (2008) revealed that the higher the level of leisure boredom that an individual experiences, the more likely he or she would be addicted to using a mobile phone. Furthermore, leisure boredom is significantly correlated with an inability to control the craving to use a mobile phone, with the accompanying loss of productivity (Leung 2008).

The literature described above suggested that if leisure time is boring and could not satisfy adolescents' expectations, they might consider the Internet as an alternative to relieve their boredom (Lin et al. 2009) and might thereby lead to addiction. Therefore, the following hypotheses are formulated:

$H_{6.1}$: Adolescents in urban China who are more leisurely bored tend to find social media more gratifying.

$H_{6.2}$: Adolescents in urban China who are more leisurely bored tend to use social media more.

$H_{6.3}$: Adolescents in urban China who are more leisurely bored are more likely to be addicted to social media.

Integrating and basing on the literature reviewed above, this study aims at identifying significant predictors for social media gratifications, level of social media use, and social media addiction. Therefore, the following research questions are raised:

RQ_6: How can demographics and sociopsychological traits of adolescents (i.e., their need for affiliation, impression management, narcissism, and leisure boredom) predict the gratifications that adolescents in urban China obtain from social media?

RQ_7: How can demographics, parental control, sociopsychological traits of adolescents, and social media gratifications predict the level of social media use among adolescents in urban China?

RQ_8: How can demographics, parental control, sociopsychological traits, gratifications, and the level of social media use discriminate social media addicts and nonaddicts among adolescents in urban China?

RQ_9: How can demographics, parental control, sociopsychological traits, gratifications, and the level of social media use predict social media addiction and the corresponding addiction symptoms among adolescents in urban China?

2.6 Impact

2.6.1 Academic Performance and Internet/Social Media Use

Researchers have long been interested in determining whether academic performance and the use of the Internet are interrelated. Some studies have examined the effects of Internet-based learning on the academic results of students.

A 16-month field study conducted by Jackson and his colleagues (2006) discovered that children from low-income families who used the Internet more had higher scores on reading achievement tests and obtained higher overall grades than children from low-income families who did not use the Internet very much. A follow-up study based on these findings concluded that academic performance can predict subsequent Internet activities and that Internet activities can predict subsequent academic performance as well (Jackson et al. 2007). In contrast, Barber (1997) reported that 86 % of teachers responding to a survey believed that Internet usage by children does not improve performance, probably because the information that the Internet contains is highly disorganized and unrelated to school curricula.

Previous research has also studied the relationship between problematic Internet use or Internet dependency and academic performance. Scherer and Bost (1997) surveyed 531 students about their Internet use, using a checklist of 10 clinical symptoms to parallel the symptoms of substance abuse and dependency. Results of this survey indicated that 13 % of the participants reported that Internet use interfered with their academic work, professional performance, or social lives. An online survey (Brenner 1997) and two campus-wide surveys conducted at the University of Texas at Austin (Scherer 1997) and Bryant College (Morahan-Martin 1997), respectively, further documented that pathological Internet use is problematic for academic performance. Scherer concluded that "excessive Internet use is problematic when it results in impaired functioning such as compromised grades or failure to fulfill responsibilities" (Scherer 1997, p. 565).

The results of a study by Mythily et al. (2008) among 2,735 adolescents in Singapore showed that excessive Internet use was associated with no rules relating to Internet use at home, fewer close friends, feelings of sadness or depression, and perceived poorer grades and school work. One study among South Korean students by Kim and his colleagues (2010) found that excessive online game playing was related to impaired academic performance. In another study among Greek college students, results also revealed that there is a significant negative relationship between Internet addiction and average marks achieved during the previous semester (Frangos 2009).

Many studies about Internet addiction and academic performance of students have been conducted in China. A recent study by Song and his colleagues (2010) among first-grade junior students in China found that the proportions of respondents demonstrating an Internet addiction tendency and the Internet addiction disorder were 10.87 % and 7.71 %, respectively. Results suggested that adolescents who suffered from poor academic performance were more likely to be addicted to Internet. Huang and his colleagues (2009) surveyed 3,496 college students from eight different universities in Wuhan, China, and found that 9.58 % were addicted to the Internet. Poor academic achievement was significantly associated with Internet addiction among the respondents. Yang (2006) discussed the impact of the Internet on moral and social aspects of youths in China and mentioned that the Internet may lead to compulsively gathering useless information and gaming for hours, adversely affecting the students' academic performance.

Similar studies were also conducted in Hong Kong. Chang and Law (2008) surveyed Hong Kong university undergraduates using Young's Internet Addiction Test and extracted three addiction dimensions: "withdrawal and social problems", "time management and performance", and "reality substitute" (p. 2609). The results also showed that academic performance was negatively correlated with the Internet addiction scores.

Researchers also tried to evaluate the relationship between social media use and academic performance. Kubey et al. (2001) revealed that heavy leisure Internet use is highly correlated with impaired academic performance, particularly when the use is with synchronous communication applications like chat rooms and Multiple User Dungeons (MUDs). The researchers proposed that the unique social qualities of such applications represent a most significant utility for otherwise lonely individuals able to stay with friends at any time. An unfortunate result is that many adolescents stay up late at night and feel tired the next day, which in turn affects their academic performances (Kubey et al. 2001).

Another study of ICQ (a specific medium of IM) was conducted in Hong Kong to examine its effects on adolescents (Cheuk and Chan 2007). The study reported that 38 % of the respondents indicated that using ICQ affected their academic performance. However, whether such effects were positive and negative could not be understood through the self-report questionnaires. Cheuk and Chan (2007) remained optimistic by concluding that if the participants used ICQ for academic issues such as discussing homework, the effect would then be positive.

Recently, Junco and his colleagues (2011) confirmed this optimistic finding by conducting an interesting semester-long experiment among college students. They separated 125 students in one course into an experimental group of 70 and a control group of 55. The experimental group used Twitter for their academic and cocurricular discussions. At the end of the semester, the authors found that the experimental group had a significantly greater increase in class engagement than the control group, as well as higher average academic scores. The authors also conducted content analysis of the Twitter messages and found that both the teacher and the students were more engaged in the learning process using Twitter than in the traditional classroom (Junco et al. 2011). This is experimental evidence that when used properly and efficiently, social media can facilitate student engagement in the learning process, thus improving academic performance.

Matthews and Schrum (2003) also confirmed this optimistic statement by studying high-speed Internet use in a college residence. They found that a positive perception of Internet use for academic performance significantly correlated with an internal locus of control for academic efforts. However, they also reported that time spent on IM was negatively associated with the ability to avoid Internet distractions and concentrate on academic tasks (Matthews and Schrum 2003).

Similarly, a study conducted by Huang and Leung (2009) on IM addiction among adolescents in China also confirmed empirically that both the level of IM use and level of IM addiction have significant and positive bivariate correlations with a decrement in academic performance. When examining the relative influence of various predictors on academic performance decrement, stepwise regression showed that four IM addiction symptoms (preoccupation with IM, loss of control, loss of relationship due to overuse, and escape) were the strongest predictors. They thus suggested that adolescents' IM use indeed affected their academic performance and that parents and teachers should pay close attention and provide proper guidance and control of adolescents' IM use (Huang and Leung 2009).

Based on the review of the above literature, the following hypotheses and research question are posed:

$H_{7.1}$: *The more the adolescents in urban China use social media, the more likely their academic performance will be affected negatively.*

$H_{7.2}$: *The more severely the adolescents in urban China are addicted to social media, the more likely their academic performance will be affected negatively.*

RQ_{10}: *Controlling for demographics, parental control, and sociopsychological traits, how can gratifications, the level of social media use, and social media addiction predict the academic performance of adolescents in urban China?*

2.6.2 Social Capital

The term social capital has been widely used to refer to the accumulated resources and benefits we receive from our social relationships (Bourdieu 2001; Lin 2001; Putnam 2000). Researchers frequently debate whether social capital is an individual or a collective phenomenon (Lin 2001). Putnam (2000) tended to view social capital as a community-level quality, while Bourdieu (2001), although conceptualizing social capital as a quality of a collective, suggested that individuals possess varying quantities of it by virtue of being qualified members of the collective. The focus of this study is on individual-level social capital.

According to Lin (2001), the instrumental notion of individual investment is central to social capital. The central premise is that individuals who pursue investment in social relations expect returns from that investment, that is, individuals engage in interactions and social networking in order to produce profits. Putnam (2000) distinguished two forms of social capital: bridging social capital and bonding social capital. Bridging social capital arises from weak ties, which are loose connections between individuals who may provide useful information to each other, but are typically lack of emotional support. Bonding social capital refers to the benefits emanating from strong or intimate ties with family and close friends. It is linked to social and emotional support as well as to substantive tangible support such as financial loans (Putnam 2000).

Ellison and his colleagues (2010) found three distinct types of findings about Internet use and social capital in the literature: (1) Internet use can increase social capital; (2) Internet use can diminish social capital; and (3) Internet use reinforces offline interactions and can supplement the development of social capital.

Past studies have investigated the relationship between social media usage and social capital. Results showed that greater use of SNS is associated with greater perceived amounts of bridging and bonding social capital (Ellison et al. 2007, 2009; Steinfield et al. 2008, 2009). In their study on the workplace, Steinfield et al. (2009), after controlling for a range of organizational demographic variables such as management level and experience in the company, found that SNS usage still associated with both dimensions of social capital. In a longitudinal study, results showed that the intensity of Facebook use in year one strongly predicted bridging social capital outcomes in year two (Steinfield et al. 2008).

Ellison et al. (2007) tried to explore another dimension of social capital, "maintained social capital," which assesses one's ability to maintain connection with members of a previously inhabited community. Results showed that after controlling for a number of factors that might explain differences in respondents' social capital, such as year in school and membership in a fraternity or sorority, the intensity of Facebook use was strongly correlated with bridging, bonding, and maintained social capital, with the strongest relationship being with bridging social capital (Ellison et al. 2007). When they explored the ways in which Facebook use contributed to social capital, Ellison et al. (2009) found that having greater numbers of "actual friends" and using SNS to interact with people known offline were predictive of both bridging and bonding social capital.

However, Valenzuela and her colleagues (2009) found that, although there were positive relationships between the intensity of Facebook use and college students' social trust, life satisfaction, civic engagement, and political participation, the associations between Facebook use and social capital was small.

Self-disclosure significantly and directly affects the bonding and bridging social capital of bloggers, which in turn enhances the perception of bloggers' subjective well-being (Ko and Kuo 2009). Bloggers share their inner feelings or moods with others through writing blogs and thus may gain social support and improve their social integration. Social capital built through blogging may improve bloggers' satisfaction with their interpersonal communication, social network, and overall quality of life (Ko and Kuo 2009).

Cohen (2007) studied the strategy of the candidate in a 2006 senate campaign to build social capital through online communities and proposed four main characteristics of the winner's digital campaign, which helped him to earn substantial social capital from his blog supporters. The four characteristics were "valuing a web presence, embracing interactivity, empowering the liberal blogosphere, and maintaining relations with the blogosphere in the post-election era" (Cohen 2007, p. 2).

Kerr (2009) suggested that social media, such as blogs and wikis, not only increase social capital for existing communities but also generate new forms of engagement and connectivity across society. Best and Krueger (2006) also found that, through IM, chat room, and online discussion groups, the online interaction people have with those they meet only online also increase their social capital, even though they do not know each other offline.

In accord with most previous studies, the social capital discussed in this study refers to overall social capital, both online and offline.

Grounded in the above literature, the following hypothesis is proposed:

$H_{8.1}$: The more the adolescents in urban China use social media, the more social capital they will have.

Although the above-mentioned studies supported the proposition that social media could increase adolescents' social capital, some research revealed that excessive online communication might decrease the user's social capital. Li and his colleagues (2009) found that, although the Internet could extend the space for adolescents' interpersonal communication, their excessive online communication could make adolescents alienated, isolated, and dissocialized, thus decreasing their social capital and even creating a pathological interpersonal mentality. Some researchers agreed with them and demonstrated that virtual online communication might attract adolescents to over indulge to escape from reality and lessen offline interpersonal communication with others. This might cause interpersonal communication disturbances in the adolescents, such as alienation, social phobia, or social anxiety, which could significantly impair their social capital (Wang and Yu 2006; Zhang and Hu 2010).

Thus, following hypothesis and research question are posed:

$H_{8.2}$: The more severely the adolescents in urban China are addicted to social media, the more likely their social capital will be decreased.

RQ_{11}: Controlling for demographics and sociopsychological traits, how can gratifications, the level of social media use, and social media addiction predict urban Chinese adolescents' social capital?

The conceptual linkages of all variables are shown in Fig. 2.1.

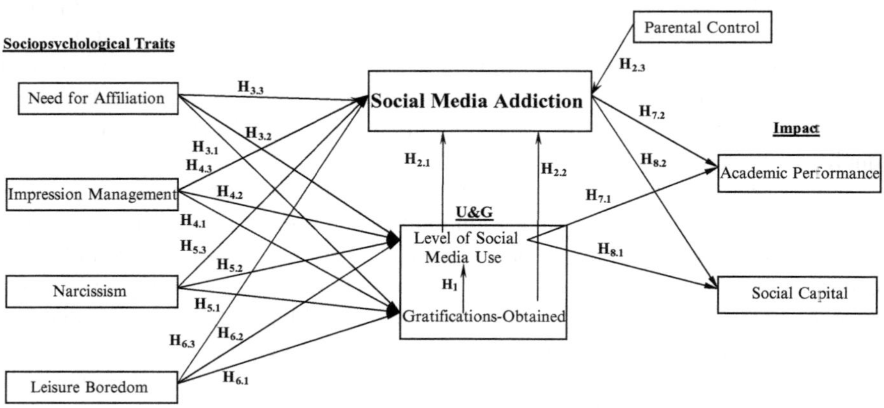

Fig. 2.1 Conceptual linkages

References

Abelman, R. (1987). Religious television uses and gratifications. *Journal of Broadcasting & Electronic Media, 31*, 293–307.

American Psychiatric Association. (1994). *Diagnostic and statistical manual for mental disorders* (4th ed.). Washington, DC: American Psychiatric Association.

Anderson, K. (1999, August). *Internet use among college students: Should we be concerned?* Paper presented at the annual conference of American Psychological Association, Boston, MA, USA.

Auter, P. J. (2007). Portable social groups: Willingness to communicate, interpersonal communication gratifications, and cell phone use among young adults. *International Journal of Mobile Communications, 5*(2), 139–156.

Ball-Rokeach, S. J., & Jung, J. Y. (2009). The evolution of media system dependency theory. In R. L. Nabi & M. B. Oliver (Eds.), *The Sage handbook of media processes and effects* (pp. 531–544). Beverly Hills: Sage Publications.

Bambooweb Dictionary. (2008). *Instant messaging.* Retrieved September 18, 2010, from http://www.bambooweb.com/articles/i/n/Instant_Messenger.html

Barber, A. (1997, March 11). Net's educational value questioned. *USA Today*, p. 4D.

Barker, O. (2009). *Five readers go on digital diet, and live to write about it.* Retrieved May 15, 2000, from http://www.usatoday.com/life/lifestyle/2009-08-02-digital-dieters_N.htm

Barnes, S. B. (2008). Understanding social media from the media ecological perspective. In E. A. Konijn, S. Utz, M. Tanis, & S. B. Barnes (Eds.), *Mediated interpersonal communication* (pp. 14–33). New York: Routledge.

Baron, R. A., & Byrne, D. (2003). *Social psychology* (10th ed.). Boston: Allyn & Bacon.

Bates, M. E. (2003). Blogs: My new addiction. *Online, 27*(5), 64

Beard, K. W. (2002). Internet addiction: Current status and implications for employees. *Journal of Employment Counseling, 39*, 2–11.

Beard, K. W., & Wolf, E. M. (2001). Modification in the proposed diagnostic criteria for Internet addiction. *CyberPsychology and Behavior, 4*(3), 377–383.

Bell, R. A., & Daly, J. A. (1984). The affinity-seeking function of communication. *Communication Monographs, 51*, 91–115.

Berelson, B. (1949). What "missing the newspaper" means. In P. F. Lazarsfeld & F. N. Stanton (Eds.), *Communication research 1948–1949* (pp. 111–129). New York: Harper.

Best, S. J., & Krueger, B. S. (2006). Online interactions and social capital distinguishing between new and existing ties. *Social Science Computer Review, 24*(4), 395–410.

Bibby, P. A. (2008). Dispositional factors in the use of social networking sites: Findings and implications for social computing research. *Lecture Notes in Computer Science, 5075*, 392–400.

Blood, R. (2002). Weblogs: A history and perspective. In J. Rodzvilla (Ed.), *We've got blog: How weblogs are changing our culture* (pp. 7–16). Cambridge, MA: Perseus.

Blumler, J. G., & Katz, E. (1974). *The uses of mass communication: Current perspectives on gratification research.* Beverly Hills: Sage.

Bolino, M. C., Kacmar, M. K., Turnley, W. H., & Gilstrap, B. J. (2008). A multi-level review of impression management motives and behaviors. *Journal of Management, 34*(6), 1080–1190.

Bourdieu, P. (2001). The forms of capital. In M. Granovetter & R. Swedberg (Eds.), *The sociology of economic life* (2nd ed., pp. 96–111). Boulder: Westview Press.

Boyatzis, R. E. (1973). Affiliation motivation: A review and a new perspective. In D. C. McClelland & R. S. Steele (Eds.), *Human motivation: A book of readings* (pp. 252–276). Morristown: General Learning Press.

Boyd, D. M. (2004, April). *Friendster and publicly articulated social networks*. Paper presented at conference on Human Factors and Computing Systems, Vienna.

Boyd, D. M., & Ellison, N. (2007). Social network sites: Definition, history, and scholarship. *Journal of Computer-Mediated Communication, 13*, 210–230.

Breakthrough Youth Research Archives. (2000). *ICQ use among adolescents in Hong Kong.* Retrieved June 25, 2008, from http://www.breakthrough.org.hk/ir/Icq/Icq.htm

Brenner, V. (1997, August). *The results of an on-line survey for the first thirty days*. Paper presented at the 105th annual meeting of the American Psychological Association, Chicago, IL, USA.
Brown, R. P., & Zeigler-Hill, V. (2004). Narcissism and the non-equivalence of self-esteem measures: A matter of dominance? *Journal of Research in Personality, 38*, 585–592.
Buffardi, L. E., & Campbell, W. K. (2008). Narcissism and social networking websites. *Personality and Social Psychology Bulletin, 34*, 1303–1314.
Caldwell, L. L., & Smith, E. A. (1995). Health behaviors of leisure alienated youth. *Society and Leisure, 18*, 143–156.
Cantril, H., & Allport, G. (1935). *The psychology of radio*. New York: Harper.
Cao, F., & Su, L. (2007). Internet addiction among Chinese adolescents: Prevalence and psychological features. *Child: Care, Health & Development, 33*(3), 275–281.
Carlson, K. S., & Gjerde, P. F. (2009). Preschool personality antecedents of narcissism in adolescence and young adulthood: A 20-year longitudinal study. *Journal of Research in Personality, 43*(4), 570–578.
Castells, M. (2000). *The rise of network society*. Oxford: Blackwell Publishers.
Chak, K., & Leung, L. (2004). Shyness and locus of control as predictors of Internet addiction and Internet use. *CyberPsychology & Behavior, 7*(5), 559–570.
Chang, M. K., & Law, S. P. M. (2008). Factors structure for Young's Internet addiction test: A confirmatory study. *Computers in Human Behavior, 24*(6), 2597–2619.
Charney, T., & Greenberg, B. S. (2002). Uses and gratifications of the Internet. In C. Lin & D. Atkin (Eds.), *Communication, technology and society: New media adoption and uses* (pp. 379–407). Cresskill: Hampton Press.
Chen, G. M. (2011). Tweet this: A uses and gratifications perspective on how active Twitter use gratifies a need to connect with others. *Computers in Human Behavior, 27*(2), 755–762.
Chester, A. (2004). *Presenting the self in cyberspace: Identity play in MOOS*. PhD thesis, Department of Philosophy. University of Melbourne, Melbourne, Australia.
Cheuk, W. S., & Chan, Z. C. Y. (2007). ICQ (I Seek You) and adolescents: A quantitative study in Hong Kong. *CyberPsychology & Behavior, 10*(1), 108–114.
Cheung, L. M., & Wong, W. S. (2011). The effects of insomnia and Internet addiction on depression in Hong Kong adolescents: An exploratory cross-sectional analysis. *Journal of Sleep Research, 20*(2), 311–317.
Cheung, C. M., Chiu, P. Y., & Lee, M. K. (2011). Online social networks: Why do students use facebook? *Computers in Human Behavior, 27*, 1337–1343.
China Youth Internet Association (CYIA). (2010). *China youth Internet addiction report*. Retrieved May 16, 2011, from http://mat1.gtimg.com/edu/pdf/wangyinbaogao.pdf
Chung, D., & Nam, C. S. (2007). An analysis of the variables predicting instant messenger use. *New Media & Society, 9*(2), 212–234.
CNNIC. (2010). *2009 research report of China youth Internet behaviors*. Retrieved September 18, 2010, from http://www.cnnic.net.cn/html/Dir/2010/04/23/5814.htm
CNNIC. (2011). *The 27th statistical survey report on Internet development in China*. Retrieved April 20, 2011, from http://www.cnnic.net.cn/dtygg/dtgg/201101/P020110119328960192287.pdf
Cohen, D. T. (2007, August). *Building social capital through online communities: The strategy of Ned Lamont's 2006 senate campaign*. Paper presented at the annual meeting of American Political Science Association, Chicago, IL, USA.
Comm, J. (2010). *Twitter power 2.0: How to dominate your market one tweet at a time*. Hoboken: Wiley.
Correa, T., Hinsley, A. W., & de Zuniga, H. G. (2010). Who interacts on the web?: The intersection of users' personality and social media use. *Computers in Human Behavior, 26*, 247–253.
Dimmick, J., Kline, S., & Stafford, L. (2000). The gratification niches of personal email and the telephone. *Communication Research, 27*(2), 227–248.
Dominick, J. R. (1999). Who do you think you are? Personal home pages and self-presentation on the World Wide Web. *Journal of Mass Communication, 76*(4), 646–658.

Donohew, L., Palmgreen, P., & Rayburn, J. D., II. (1987). Social and psychological origins of media use: A lifestyle analysis. *Journal of Broadcasting & Electronic Media, 31*, 255–278.

Dozier, D. M., & Rice, R. E. (1984). Rival theories of electronic newsgathering. In R. E. Rice (Ed.), *The new media: Communication, research, and technology* (pp. 103–128). Beverly Hills: Sage.

Dunne, A., & Lawlor, M. (2010). Young people's use of online social networking sites—A uses and gratifications perspective. *Journal of Research in Interactive Marketing, 4*(1), 46–58.

Eighmey, J., & McCord, L. (1998). Adding value in the information age: Uses and gratifications of sites on the World Wide Web. *Journal of Business Research, 51*, 187–194.

Elliott, R., Eccles, S., & Gournay, K. (1996). Revenge, existential choice, and addictive consumption. *Psychology and Marketing, 13*, 753–768.

Ellison, N., Heino, R., & Gibbs, J. (2006). Managing impressions online: Self-presentation processes in the online dating environment. *Journal of Computer-Mediated Communication, 11*, 415–441.

Ellison, N., Steinfield, C., & Lampe, C. (2007). The benefits of Facebook "friends": Exploring the relationship between college students' use of online social networks and social capital. *Journal of Computer-Mediated Communication, 12*(4), 1143–1168.

Ellison, N., Steinfield, C., & Lampe, C. (2009, May). *Connection strategies: Relationship formation and maintenance on social network sites.* Paper presented at the annual meeting of the International Communication Association, Chicago, IL, USA.

Ellison, N., Lampe, C., Steinfield, C., & Vitak, J. (2010). With a little help from my friends: How social network sites affect social capital processes. In Z. Papacharissi (Ed.), *The networked self: Identity, community, and culture on social network sites* (pp. 124–146). New York: Routledge.

Ferguson, D., & Perse, E. (2000). The World Wide Web as a functional alterative to television. *Journal of Broadcasting & Electronic Media, 44*(2), 155–174.

Ferraro, G., Caci, B., D'Amico, A., & Blasi, M. D. (2007). Internet addiction disorder: An Italian study. *CyberPsychology & Behavior, 10*(2), 170–175.

Frangos, C. C. (2009). Internet dependence in college student from Greece. *European Psychiatry, 24*, S419.

Funk, J. B., & Buchman, D. D. (1996). Playing violent video and computer games and adolescent self-concept. *Journal of Communication, 46*(2), 19–32.

Gable, S. L. (2006). Approach and avoidance social motives and goals. *Journal of Personality, 74*(1), 175–223.

Geng, Y., Su, L., & Cao, F. (2006). A research on emotion and personality characteristics in junior 1 high school students with internet addiction disorders. *Chinese Journal of Clinical Psychology, 14*, 153–155.

Ghassemzadeh, L., Shahraray, M., & Moradi, A. (2008). Prevalence of Internet addiction and comparison of Internet addicts and non-addicts in Iranian high schools. *CyberPsychology & Behavior, 11*(6), 731–733.

Gibbs, J., Ellison, N., & Heino, R. (2006). Self-presentation in online personals: The role of anticipated future interaction, self-disclosure, and perceived success in Internet dating. *Communication Research, 33*, 152–180.

Gilmore, D. C., Stevens, C. K., Harrell-Cook, G., & Ferris, G. R. (1999). Impression management tactics. In R. W. Eder & M. M. Harris (Eds.), *The employment interview handbook* (pp. 321–336). London: Sage.

Goffman, E. (1959). *The presentation of self in everyday life*. New York: Penguin.

Gong, J., Chen, X., Zeng, J., Li, F., Zhou, D., & Wang, Z. (2009). Adolescent addictive Internet use and drug abuse in Wuhan, China. *Addiction Research & Theory, 17*(3), 291–305.

Griffiths, M. D. (1996). Gambling on the Internet: A brief note. *Journal of Gambling Studies, 12*, 471–473.

Griffiths, M. D. (1998). Internet addiction: Does it really exist? In J. Gackenbach (Ed.), *Psychology and the Internet: Intrapersonal, interpersonal, and transpersonal applications* (pp. 61–75). New York: Academic.

Griffiths, M. D. (2000). Does Internet and "addiction" exist? Some case study evidence. *CyberPsychology and Behavior, 3*, 211–218.

Griffiths, M. D., & Hunt, N. (1998). Dependence on computer games by adolescents. *Psychology Reports, 82*, 475–480.

Haddock, B. D., & Beto, D. R. (1988). Assessment of drug and alcohol problems: A probation model. *Federal Probation, 52*, 10–16.

Harter, S. (1999). *The construction of the self: A developmental perspective*. New York: Guilford.

Harter, S. (2006). The self. In W. Damon & R. M. Lerner (Series Eds.) & N. Eisenberg (Vol. Ed.), *Handbook of child psychology: Vol. 3. Social, emotional, and personality development* (pp. 505–570). New York: Wiley.

Herzog, H. (1944). What do we really know about daytime serial listeners? In P. F. Lazarsfeld & F. N. Stanton (Eds.), *Radio research 1942–1943* (pp. 3–33). New York: Duell, Sloan & Pearce.

Hill, A. B., & Perkins, R. E. (1985). Towards a model of boredom. *British Journal of Psychology, 76*, 235–240.

Honeycutt, C., & Herring, S. C. (2009). Beyond microblogging: Conversation and collaboration via Twitter. In: *Proceedings of the forty-second Hawaii International Conference on System Sciences (HICSS-42)*. Los Alamitos: IEEE Press.

Huang, H. (2008, July). *Instant messenger use among teenagers in China: Motives, shyness, alienation, and social support.* Paper presented at the annual conference of International Association for Media and Communication Research Conference, Stockholm, Sweden.

Huang, H., & Leung, L. (2009). Instant messaging addiction among teenagers in China: Shyness, alienation, and academic performance decrement. *CyberPsychology & Behavior, 12*(6), 675–679.

Huang, L., Chou, Y., & Lin, C. (2008). In influence of reading motives on the responses after reading blogs. *CyberPsychology & Behavior, 11*(3), 351–355.

Huang, R. L., Lu, Z., Liu, J. J., You, Y. M., Pan, Z. Q., Wei, Z., He, Q., & Wang, Z. Z. (2009). Features and predictors of problematic Internet use in Chinese college students. *Behavior & Information Technology, 28*(5), 485–590.

Huang, X., Zhang, H., Li, M., Wang, J., Zhang, Y., & Tao, R. (2010). Mental health, personality, and parental rearing styles of adolescents with Internet addiction disorder. *Cyberpsychology, Behavior and Social Networking, 13*(4), 401–406.

Hwang, H. (2009, May). *Predictors of instant messaging: Gratifications sought, gratifications obtained, and social presence.* Paper presented at the annual meeting of the International Communication Association, New York City, NY.

Iso-Ahola, S. E., & Crowley, E. D. (1991). Adolescent substance abuse and leisure boredom. *Journal of Leisure Research, 23*(3), 260–271.

Iso-Ahola, S. E., & Weissinger, E. (1990). Perceptions of boredom in leisure: Conceptualization, reliability and validity of the leisure boredom scale. *Journal of Leisure Research, 22*(1), 1–17.

Jackson, A., von Eye, A., Biocca, F., Barbatsis, G., Zhao, Y., & Fitzergald, H. (2006). Does home Internet use influence the academic performance of low-income children? *Developmental Psychology, 42*(3), 429–435.

Jackson, A., Samona, R., Moomaw, J., Ramsay, L., Murray, C., Smith, A., & Murray, L. (2007). What children do on the Internet: Domains visited and their relationship to socio-demographic characteristics and academic performance. *CyberPsychology & Behavior, 10*(2), 182–190.

Jacobs, R. (1995). Exploring the determinants of cable television subscriber satisfaction. *Journal of Broadcasting & Electronic Media, 39*, 262–274.

James, M. L., Wotring, C. E., & Forrest, E. J. (1995). An exploratory study of the perceived benefits of electronic bulletin board use and their impact on other communication activities. *Journal of Broadcasting & Electronic Media, 39*, 30–50.

Java, A., Song, X., Finin, T., & Tseng, B. (2007, August). *Why we twitter: Understanding microblogging usage and communities.* Paper presented at Joint 9th WEBKDD and 1st SNA-KDD workshop, San Jose, CA, USA.

Johnson, P. R., & Yang, S. (2009, August). *Uses and gratifications of Twitter: An examination of users' motives and satisfaction of Twitter use.* Paper presented at the Communication

Technology Division of the annual convention of the Association for Education in Journalism and Mass Communication, Boston, MA, USA.

Joinson, A. N. (2003). *Understanding the psychology of Internet behavior: Virtual worlds, real lives*. Basingstoke/New York: Palgrave Macmillan.

Jones, E. E., & Pittman, T. S. (1982). Toward a general theory of strategic self-presentation. In J. Suls (Ed.), *Psychological perspectives on the self* (Vol. 1, pp. 231–262). Hillsdale: Lawrence Erlbaum.

Junco, R., Heibergert, G., & Loken, E. (2011). The effect of Twitter on college student engagement and grades. *Journal of Computer Assisted Learning, 27*, 119–132.

Jung, T., Youn, H., & McClung, S. (2007). Motivations and self-presentation strategies on Korean-based "Cyworld" weblog format personal homepages. *CyberPsychology and Behavior, 10*(1), 24–31.

Kaplan, A. M., & Haenlein, M. (2010). Users of the world, unite! The challenges and opportunities of social media. *Business Horizons, 53*(1), 59–68.

Karaiskos, D., Tzavellas, E., Balta, G., & Paparrigopoulos, T. (2010). Social network addiction: A new clinical disorder? *European Psychiatry, 25*(Supplement 1), 855.

Katz, E., & Foulkes, D. (1962). On the use of mass media as escape: Clarification of a concept. *Public Opinion Quarterly, 26*, 377–388.

Katz, E., Blumler, J. G., & Gurevitch, M. (1974). Utilization of mass communication by the individual. In J. D. Blumler & E. Katz (Eds.), *The uses of mass communications: Current perspectives on gratifications research* (pp. 19–32). Beverly Hills: Sage.

Kernberg, O. (1975). *Borderline conditions and pathological narcissism*. New York: Aronson.

Kerr, J. (2009, April). *Surging together: A preliminary inquiry into the effects of Internet use on social capital in American communities*. Paper presented at the annual meeting of Midwestern Political Science Association, Chicago, IL, USA.

Kim, J. W., Han, D. H., Park, D. B., Min, K. J., Na, C., Won, S. K., & Park, G. N. (2010). The relationships between online game player biogenetic traits, playing time, and the genre of the game being played. *Psychiatry Investigation, 7*(1), 17–23.

Klapper, J. T. (1963). Mass communication research: An old road resurveyed. *Public Opinion Quarterly, 27*, 515–527.

Kleck, C. A., Reese, C., Ziegerer-Behnken, D., & Sandar, S. (2007). *The company you keep and the image you project: Putting your best face forward in online social networks*. Paper presented at the annual meeting of the International Communication Association, San Francisco, CA, USA.

Ko, H., & Kuo, F. (2009). Can blogging enhance subjective well-being through self-disclosure? *CyberPsychology & Behavior, 12*(1), 75–79.

Ko, C. H., Yen, J. Y., Yen, C. F., Lin, H. C., & Yang, M. J. (2007). Factors predictive for incidence and remission of Internet addiction in young adolescents: A prospective study. *CyberPsychology & Behavior, 10*(4), 545–551.

Ko, C. H., Yen, J. Y., Yen, C. F., Chen, C. S., Weng, C. C., & Chen, C. C. (2008). The association between Internet addiction and problematic alcohol use in adolescents: The problem behavior model. *Cyberpsychology & Behavior, 11*(5), 571–576.

Kramer, N. C., & Winter, S. (2008). Impression management 2.0. The relationship of self-esteem, extraversion, self-efficacy, and self-presentation within social network sites. *Journal of Media Psychology, 20*(3), 106–116.

Kubey, R., Lavin, M. J., & Barrows, J. R. (2001). Internet use and collegiate academic performance decrements: Early findings. *Journal of Communication, 51*(2), 366–382.

Lam, L., Peng, Z., Mai, J., & Jing, J. (2009). Factors associated with Internet addiction among adolescents. *CyberPsychology & Behavior, 12*(5), 551–555.

Lansing, J. B., & Heyns, R. W. (1959). Need for affiliation and frequency of four types of communication. *Journal of Abnormal and Social Psychology, 58*(3), 365–372.

LaPorta, L. (2009). Twitter and YouTube: Unexpected consequences of the self-esteem movement? *Psychiatric Times, 26*(11), 1–8.

LaRose, R., & Atkin, D. (1991). An analysis of pay-per-view versus other movie delivery modalities. *Journal of Media Economics, 4*, 3–17.

Lasswell, H. D. (1948). The structure and function of communication in society. In L. Bryson (Ed.), *The communication of ideas: A series of addresses* (pp. 37–51). New York: Harper.
Leary, M. R. (1996). *Self-presentation: Impression management and interpersonal behavior*. Boulder: Westview Press.
Lee, D., Im, S., & Taylor, C. (2008). Voluntary self-disclosure of information on the Internet: A multimethod study of the motivations and consequences of disclosing information on blogs. *Psychology & Marketing, 25*(7), 692–710.
Lemish, D. (1985). Soap opera viewing in college: A naturalistic inquiry. *Journal of Broadcasting & Electronic Media, 29*, 275–293.
Lemon, J. (2002). Can we call behaviors addictive? *Clinical Psychologist, 6*, 44–49.
Lenhart, A. (2009). *Pew Internet and American Life Project: Adults and social network web sites.* Retrieved September 19, 2010, from http://www.pewinternet.org/Reports/2009/Adults-and-Social-Network-Websites.aspx/
Lenhart, A., Rainie L., & Lewis O. (2001). *Teenage life online* (report).Washington, DC: Pew Internet & American Life Project.
Leung, L. (2001). College student motives for chatting on ICQ. *New Media and Society, 3*(4), 483–500.
Leung, L. (2002). Loneliness, self-disclosure, and ICQ use. *CyberPsychology & Behavior, 5*(3), 241–251.
Leung, L. (2003). Impacts of net-generation attributes, seductive properties of the Internet, and gratifications-obtained on Internet use. *Telematics & Informatics, 20*(2), 107–129.
Leung, L. (2004). Net-generation attributes and seductive properties of the Internet as predictors of online activities and Internet addiction. *CyberPsychology & Behavior, 7*(3), 333–348.
Leung, L. (2007). Unwillingness to communication and college students' motives in SMS mobile messaging. *Telematics and Informatics, 24*(2), 115–129.
Leung, L. (2008). Leisure boredom, sensation seeking, self-esteem, addiction symptoms and patterns of mobile phone use. In E. Korini, S. Utz, M. Tanis, & S. B. Barnes (Eds.), *Mediated interpersonal communication*. New York: Routledge.
Leung, L. (2009). Users-generated content on the Internet: An examination of gratifications, civic engagement, and psychological empowerment. *New Media & Society, 11*(8), 1327–1347.
Leung, L., & Wei, R. (2000). More than just talk on the move: Uses and gratifications of cellular phone. *Journalism and Mass Communication Quarterly, 77*(2), 308–320.
Levy, M. R., & Windahl, S. (1984). Audience activity and gratifications: A conceptual clarification and exploration. *Communication Research, 11*, 51–78.
Li, X., Li, Z., & Xie, W. (2006). Epidemiological investigation on internet addiction among middle school students in Hefei. *Chinese Mental Health Journal, 20*, 51–54.
Li, C., Liu, J., Guo, S., Zhang, W., Fang, Z., & Jiang, H. (2009). Analyses of Internet use among college students. *Journal of Dalian University of Technology (Social Sciences), 30*(3), 104–107.
Liang, N. J. (2006). The assessment and intervention of adolescents' Internet addiction. In Shanghai Youth Association (Ed.), *The Internet addiction among youth and the interventions* (pp. 43–55). Shanghai: East China University of Science and Technology Press.
Lin, C. A. (1993). Exploring the role of the VCR use in the emerging home entertainment culture. *Journalism Quarterly, 70*, 833–842.
Lin, C. A. (1996). Looking back: The contribution of Blumler and Katz's uses and mass communication to communication research. *Journal of Broadcasting & Electronic Media, 40*, 574–581.
Lin, N. (2001). Building a network theory of social capital. In N. Lin, K. Cook, & R. Burt (Eds.), *Social capital theory and research* (pp. 3–30). New Brunswick: Transaction Publishers.
Lin, C. H., & Yu, S. F. (2008). Adolescent Internet usage in Taiwan: Exploring gender differences. *Adolescence, 43*(170), 317–331.
Lin, C., Lin, S., & Wu, C. (2009). The effects of parental monitoring and leisure boredom on adolescents' Internet addiction. *Adolescence, 44*(176), 993–1004.
Liu, Y. (2007). Psycho-social related factors of junior high school students with Internet addiction disorder. *Chinese Journal of Clinical Psychology, 15*, 422–423.

Liu, C. Y., & Kuo, F. Y. (2007). A study of Internet addiction through the lens of the interpersonal theory. *Cyberpsychology & Behavior, 10*(6), 799–804.

Ljungstrand, P., & Segerstad, Y. H. (2000). Awareness of presence, instant messaging and webwho. *Siggroup Bulletin, 21*(3), 21–27.

Mansikka, J. (2009). Can boredom educate us? Tracing a mood in Heidegger's fundamental ontology from an educational point of view. *Studies in Philosophy & Education, 28*, 255–268.

Marsh, H., Craven, R. G., & Debus, R. L. (1998). Structure, stability, and development of young children's self-concepts: A multicohort-multioccasion study. *Child Development, 69*, 1030–1053.

Martinez, H. (2009, January 23). Tweet this: Southeast Texans microblog every day happenings and more. *Beaumont Enterprise.*

Marwick, A. (2005, October). *I'm a lot more interesting than a Friendster profile: Identity, authenticity, and power in social networking services.* Paper presented at the conference of Association for Internet Researchers 6, Chicago, IL, USA.

Matthews, D., & Schrum, L. (2003). High-speed Internet use and academic gratifications in the college residence. *Internet & Higher Education, 6*(2), 125–144.

Mattick, R. P., & Baillie, A. (1992). *National campaign against drug abuse: An outlet for approaches to smoking cessation* (Monograph No. 19). Canberra: Australian Government Publishing Service.

McClelland, D. C. (1976). *The achieving society: With a new introduction.* New York: Irvington.

McIlwraith, R. D. (1998). "I'm addicted to television": The personality, imagination, and TV watching patterns of self-identified TV addicts. *Journal of Broadcasting & Electronic Media, 42*, 371–386.

McKenna, K. Y. A., Green, A. S., & Gleason, M. E. J. (2002). Relationship formation on the Internet. What's the big attraction? *Journal of Social Issues, 58*(1), 9–31.

McLeod, J. M., Bybee, C. R., & Durall, J. A. (1982). On evaluating news media performance. *Political Communication, 10*, 16–22.

Mendelsohn, H. (1964). Listening to the radio. In L. A. Dexter & D. M. White (Eds.), *People, society and mass communication* (pp. 239–248). New York: Free Press.

Miller, A. (1981). *The drama of the gifted child.* New York: Basic Books.

Miller, A. (1985). *For your own good.* New York: Farrar, Straus & Giroux.

Miller, W. R. (2006). Motivational factors in addictive behaviors. In W. R. Miller & K. M. Carroll (Eds.), *Rethinking substance abuse: What the science shows* (pp. 136–150). New York: Guilford Press.

Millon, T. (1981). *Disorders of personality.* New York: Wiley.

Mnookin, J. (1996). Virtual(ly) law: The emergence of law in LambdaMOO. *Journal of Computer-Mediated Communication, 2*(1), no page indicated.

Morahan-Martin, J. (1997, August). *Incidence and correlates of pathological Internet use.* Paper presented at the 105th annual meeting of the American Psychological Association, Chicago, IL, USA.

Morf, C. C., & Rhodewalt, F. (2001). Unraveling the paradoxes of narcissism: A dynamic self-regulatory processing model. *Psychological Inquiry, 12*, 177–196.

Murphy. D. (2005). A virtual student body: A behind-the-scenes look at Facebook.com, the college world's most popular online social network. *PC Magazine*, p. 82.

Murphy, J. (2008). Better practices from the field: Micro-blogging for science & technology libraries. *Science & Technology Libraries, 28*, 4.

Murray, H. A. (1938). *Explorations in personality.* New York: Oxford University Press.

Mythily, S., Qiu, S., & Winslow, M. (2008). Prevalence and correlates of excessive Internet use among youth in Singapore. *Annals of the Academy of Medicine, Singapore, 37*(1), 9–14.

OECD. (2007). *Participative web and user-created content: Web 2.0, wikis, and social networking.* Paris: Organization for Economic Co-operation and Development.

Oravec, J. A. (2002). Bookmarking the world: Weblog application in education. *Journal of Adolescent and Adult Literacy, 45*, 622–625.

Orford, J. (2001). *Excessive appetites: A psychological view of addictions* (2nd ed.). Chichester: Wiley.

Palmgreen, P., & Rayburn, J. D., II. (1979). Uses and gratifications and exposure to public television. *Communication Research, 6*, 155–180.

Papacharissi, Z., & Rubin, A. M. (2000). Predictors of Internet use. *Journal of Broadcasting & Electronic Media, 44*, 175–196.

Park, W. K. (2005). Mobile phone addiction. In R. Ling & P. E. Pedersen (Eds.), *Mobile communication: Re-negotiation of the social sphere*. London: Springer.

Park, N., Kee, K. F., & Valenzuela, S. (2009). Being immersed in social networking environment: Facebook groups, uses and gratifications, and social outcomes. *CyberPsychology & Behavior, 12*(6), 729–733.

Peele, S. (1985). *The meaning of addiction*. Lexington: Lexington Books.

Perse, E. M., & Dunn, D. G. (1998). The utility of home computers and media use: Implications of multimedia and connectivity. *Journal of Broadcasting & Electronic Media, 42*, 435–456.

Perse, E. M., & Ferguson, D. A. (2000). The benefits and costs of web surfing. *Communication Quarterly, 48*(4), 343–359.

Peter, J., & Valkenburg, P. M. (2006). Research note: Individual differences in perceptions of Internet communication. *European Journal of Communication, 21*(2), 213–226.

Peters, O., & Allouch, S. B. (2005). Always connected: A longitudinal field study of mobile communication. *Telecommunications Policy, 22*, 239–256.

Pettersson, T. (1986). The audiences' uses and gratifications of TV worship services. *Journal for the Scientific Study of Religion, 25*, 391–409.

Phillips, A. (1993). *On kissing, tickling, and being bored: Psychoanalytic essays on the unexamined life*. Cambridge, MA: Harvard University Press.

Pinsky, D., & Young, S. M. (2009). *The mirror effect: How celebrity narcissism is seducing America*. New York: HarperCollins Publishers.

Putnam, R. D. (2000). *Bowling alone: The collapse and revival of American community*. New York: Simon & Schuster.

Quan-Haase, A., & Young, A. L. (2010). Bulletin of science. *Technology & Society, 30*(5), 350–361.

Raacke, J., & Bonds-Raacke, J. (2008). MySpace and Facebook: Applying the uses and gratifications theory to exploring friend-networking sites. *CyberPsychology & Behavior, 11*(2), 169–174.

Rafaeli, S. (1986). The electronic bulletin board: A computer-driven mass medium. *Computers and the Social Sciences, 2*, 123–136.

Ramirez, A., & Broneck, K. (2003). *IM me: Instant messaging as relational maintenance and everyday communication*. Paper presented at annual meeting of International Communication Association, San Diego, CA, USA.

Ramirez, A., Dimmick, J., Feaster, J., & Lin, S. (2008). Revisiting interpersonal media competition—The gratification niches of instant messaging, email, and the telephone. *Communication Research, 35*(4), 529–547.

Recchiuti, J. K. (2003). *College students' uses and motives for email, instant messaging, and online chat rooms*. Unpublished master's thesis. University of Delaware, Newark, DE, USA.

Riva, G. (2002). The sociocognitive psychology of computer-mediated communication: The present and future of technology-based interactions. *CyberPsychology & Behavior, 5*, 581–598.

Rosenberg, J. (2009). *Online impression management: Personality traits and concern for secondary goals as predictors of self-presentation tactics on Facebook*. Unpublished master's thesis. Kent State University, Kent, OH, USA.

Rosengren, K. E. (1974). Uses and gratifications: A paradigm outlined. In J. G. Blumler & E. Katz (Eds.), *The uses of mass communication—Current perspectives on gratifications research* (pp. 269–286). London: Sage.

Rubin, A. M. (1979). Television use by children and adolescents. *Human Communication Research, 5*, 355–369.

Rubin, A. M. (1984). Ritualized and instrumental television viewing. *Journal of Communication, 34*(3), 67–77.

Rubin, A. M. (2002). The uses-and-gratifications perspective of media effects. In J. Bryant & D. Zillmann (Eds.), *Media effects: Advances in theory and research* (pp. 525–548). Mahwah: Erlbaum.

Ruggiero, T. E. (2000). Uses and gratifications theory in the 21s century. *Mass Communication & Society, 3*(1), 3–37.

Scherer, K. (1997). College life online: Healthy and unhealthy Internet use. *Journal of College Life and Development, 38*(6), 655–665.

Scherer, K., & Bost, J. (1997, August). *Internet use patterns: Is there Internet dependency on campus?* Paper presented at the 105th annual convention of the American Psychological Association, Chicago, IL, USA.

Schlenker, B. R. (1980). *Impression management: The self-concept, social identity, and interpersonal relationships*. Monterey: Brooks/Cole.

Schneider, D. J. (1981). Tactical self-representations toward a broader conception. In J. Tedeschi (Ed.), *Impression management theory and social psychological research* (pp. 23–40). New York: Academic.

Schramm, W. (1949). The nature of news. *Journalism Quarterly, 26*, 259–269.

Schuckit, M. A. (1987). Biological vulnerability to alcoholism. *Journal of Consulting and Clinical Psychology, 55*, 301–309.

Shaffer, H. J. (1996). Understanding the means and objects of addiction: Technology, the Internet and gambling. *Journal of Gambling Studies, 12*, 461–469.

Shaver, J. L. (1983). *The uses of cable television.* Unpublished masters thesis, University of Kentucky, Lexington, KY, USA.

Shotton, M. A. (1989). *Computer addiction?: A study of computer dependency*. London: Taylor & Francis.

Siomos, K. E., Dafouli, E. D., Braimiotis, D. A., Mouzas, O. D., & Angelopoulos, N. V. (2008). Internet addiction among Greek adolescent students. *CyberPsychology & Behavior, 11*(6), 653–657.

Song, I., LaRose, R., Eastin, M. S., & Lin, C. A. (2004). Internet gratifications and Internet addiction: On the uses and abuses of new media. *CyberPsychology & Behavior, 7*(4), 384–394.

Song, X. Q., Zheng, L., Li, Y., Yu, D. X., & Wang, Z. Z. (2010). Status of Internet addiction disorder and its risk factors among first-grade junior students in Wuhan. *Zhonghua Liu Xing Bing Xue Za Zhi, 31*(1), 14–17.

Spannerworks. (2007). *What is social media?* Retrieved April 20, 2011, from http://www.icrossing.co.uk/fileadmin/uploads/eBooks/What_is_Social_Media_iCrossing_ebook.pdf

Stafford, T. F., & Stafford, M. R. (2004). Determining uses and gratifications. *Decision Science, 35*(2), 259–288.

Steinfield, C., Ellison, N., & Lampe, C. (2008). Social capital, self-esteem, and use of online social network sites: A longitudinal analysis. *Journal of Applied Developmental Psychology, 29*(6), 434–445.

Steinfield, C., DiMicco, J. M., Ellison, N. B., & Lampe, C. (2009). Bowling online: Social networking and social capital within the organization. In *Proceedings of the fourth international conference on communities and technologies* (pp. 245–254). New York: ACM.

Tao, R., Ying, L., Yue, X., & Hao, X. (2007). *Internet addiction: Exploration and interventions.* Shanghai: Century Publishing Group.

Tedeschi, J. T., & Riess, M. (1981). Identities, the phenomenal self, and laboratory research. In J. T. Tedeschi (Ed.), *Impression management theory and social psychology research* (pp. 3–22). New York: Academic.

Trammell, K. D., Tarkowski A., & Hofmokl, J. (2004, September). *Republic of blog.* Paper presented at the 5th annual meeting of the Association of Internet Researchers, Brighton, UK.

Tsai, C. C., & Lin, S. J. (2003). Internet addiction of adolescents in Taiwan: An interview study. *CyberPsychology & Behavior, 6*, 649–652.

Twenge, J. M., & Campbell, W. K. (2009). *The narcissism epidemic: Living in the age of entitlement*. New York: Free Press.

Urista, M. A., Dong, Q., & Day, K. D. (2009). Explaining why young adults use MySpace and Facebook through uses and gratification theory. *Human Communication, 12*(2), 215–229.

Valenzuela, S., Park, N., & Kee, K. F. (2009). Is there social capital in a social network site?: Facebook use and college students' life satisfaction, trust, and participation. *Journal of Computer-Mediated Communication, 14*, 875–901.
Veroff, J., Reuman, D., & Feld, S. (1984). Motive in American men and women across the adult life span. *Developmental Psychology, 20*, 1142–1158.
Walther, J. B. (1993). Impression development in computer-mediated interaction. *Western Journal of Communication, 57*, 381–398.
Walther, J. B., Slovacek, C. L., & Tidwell, L. C. (2001). Is a picture worth a thousand words? Photographic images in long-term and short-term computer-mediated communication. *Communication Research, 28*, 105–134.
Wang, Y., & Fesenmaier, D. (2004). Modeling participation in an online travel community. *Journal of Travel Research, 42*, 261–270.
Wang, H., & Yu, Z. (2006). The characteristics of Internet and its cause to adolescents' delinquency. *Journal of Jilin Public Security Academy, 21*(3), 41–54.
Wei, R., & Lo, V. H. (2006). Staying connected while on the move: Cell phone use and social connectedness. *New Media & Society, 8*(1), 53–72.
Wellman, B. (1996). An electronic group is virtually a social network. In S. Kiesler (Ed.), *Culture of the Internet* (pp. 179–205). Hillsdale: Lawrence Erlbaum.
Wimmer, R. D., & Dominick, J. R. (1994). *Mass media research: An introduction.* Belmont: Wadsworth.
Wolfe, K. M., & Fiske, M. (1949). The children talk about comics. In P. F. Lazarsfeld & F. N. Stanton (Eds.), *Communications research, 1948–1949* (pp. 3–50). New York: Harper & Brothers.
Wright, C. (1960). Functional analysis and mass communication. *Public Opinion Quarterly, 24*, 605–620.
Yang, S. (2006). An informal discussion on Internet matters. *Chinese Education & Society, 39*(1), 65.
Yang, S. C., & Tung, C. J. (2007). Comparison of Internet addicts and non-addicts in Taiwanese high school. *Computer in Human Behavior, 23*(1), 79–96.
Yen, J., Yen, C., Chen, C., Chen, S., & Ko, C. (2007). Family factors of Internet addiction and substance use experience in Taiwanese adolescents. *CyberPsychology & Behavior, 10*(3), 323–329.
Young, K. S. (1996). *Caught in the net: How to recognize the signs of internet addiction—and a winning strategy for recovery*. New York: Wiley.
Young, K. S. (1998). Internet addiction: The emergence of a new clinical disorder. *CyberPsychology & Behavior, 1*, 237–244.
Young, K. S. (1999). Internet addiction: Symptoms, evaluation, and treatment. In L. VandeCreek & T. Jackson (Eds.), *Innovations in clinical practice: A source book* (Vol. 17, pp. 19–31). Sarasota: Professional Resource Press.
Yuen, C. N., & Lavin, M. J. (2004). Internet dependence in the collegiate population: The role of shyness. *CyberPsychology & Behavior, 7*(4), 379–383.
Zhang, Y., & Hu, J. (2010). The impact of Internet culture on college students' interpersonal competence. *Economic and Social Development, 8*(6), 177–179.
Zhao, C. (2010). *Children beside windows: The family factors of game addiction.* Zhejiang: Zhejiang University Press.
Zhou, Y. (2009). Behavioral versus perceptional dimensions of Social Networking Websites use and their relationship to young adults' social motives, personality, and social well-being. *China Computer-Mediated Communication Studies, 3*, 27–46.
Ziervogel, C. F., Ahmed, N., Flisher, A. J., & Robertson, B. A. (1998). Alcohol misuse in South African male adolescents: A qualitative investigation. *International Quarterly of Community Health Education, 17*, 25–41.

Chapter 3
Research Methods

In this chapter, the research methods used for this study are discussed in detail. The chapter first introduces the data collection procedure. As the main research method in this study, the questionnaire survey is then elaborated in detail, on survey participants, sites of the study, pilot tests, the sampling procedure, final sample profiles, measures and the reliability of the scales, as well as the analytical procedure. Focus groups and in-depth interviews are also discussed.

3.1 Data Collection Procedure

To provide a comprehensive understanding of social media addiction among adolescents in urban China, a quantitative self-administrated questionnaire survey was executed, qualitative focus group sessions were held, and semi-structured interviews were conducted. Since the main objective of this research is to examine the general status of social media addiction among adolescents, the social and psychological antecedents, gratifications, as well as the impact of social media addiction, the questionnaire survey served as the main research method to reach the goal. Pre-survey focus group sessions were held before the actual survey to assist with the questionnaire design. After the survey, semi-structured in-depth interviews were conducted with parents and teachers of the adolescents who participated in the survey. The qualitative data gathered from these interviews served as supplements to the survey results, providing another perspective of the phenomenon of social media addiction among adolescents.

H. Huang, *Social Media Generation in Urban China: A Study of Social Media Use and Addiction among Adolescents*, Understanding China,
DOI 10.1007/978-3-642-45441-7_3, © Springer-Verlag Berlin Heidelberg 2014

3.2 Questionnaire Survey

3.2.1 Survey Participants

The word "adolescence" originated from Latin and is derived from the verb "adolescere," which means "to grow into adulthood" (Encyclopedia of Children's Health 2011). According to Violato and Travis (1995), "adolescents are those whose childhood have, with puberty, come to an end, but whose adult life have yet to begin for full adult status with its duties, obligations, and responsibilities with its prerogatives and privileges" (p. 28). It is a transitional stage between the beginning of puberty (sexual maturation) and legal adulthood, a time of moving from the immaturity of childhood into the maturity of adulthood, while physical and mental human development both occur during this period (Marcell 2007). There is no specific time or boundary indicating the end of childhood or the beginning of adolescence. However, the passage from childhood into adolescence is indicated by a set of transitions, which are biological, cognitive, social, and emotional (Encyclopedia of Children's Health 2011). According to Erik Erikson's (1950) eight stages of human development, adolescents are in the period of identity versus role confusion. Individuals become more independent, explore possibilities, and begin to form their own identity based on the outcome of their explorations in adolescence (Erikson 1950).

The adolescent population is well represented by middle-school students. Middle-school students, from Grade 7 to Grade 12, are normally between the ages of 12 and 18, which span the developmental transition between childhood and adulthood. Thus, in this study, the sampling population is middle-school students in urban China. Although Erikson (1950) suggested that adolescents usually are persons between the ages of 13 and 18, it is well recognized that the end of childhood and the beginning of adulthood do not have specific cutoff age points and always vary from country to country and culture to culture (Violato and Travis 1995). In China, most students finish primary school and enter middle school at the age of 12, which is a milestone indicating the end of childhood and the beginning of adolescence. Meanwhile, setting 12 as the beginning of adolescence also solves the problem of there being about a 1-year difference between girls and boys at the onset of puberty (Haffner 1995). In most countries, entering adulthood means the person is mature enough to be entrusted by society with certain behaviors or tasks, for example, driving, purchasing or drinking alcohol, and voting, to name a few. In China, 18 is indeed the cutoff age indicating the end of adolescence and the beginning of adulthood. Schools or many social organizations arrange adult ceremonies for those who turn 18 that year. Those who participate in adult ceremonies pledge under the national flag that they will take responsibility for themselves and society from then on. They also obtain the right to vote and acquire legal liability. The adolescent population in China is therefore well represented by middle-school students from Grade 7 to Grade 12, who are between the ages of 12 and 18.

3.2.2 Urban Chinese Cities for the Study

It is mentioned in the introduction section that, in China, adolescents in remote districts may not even have access to the Internet, let alone use social media. There would therefore be scarcely any social media addiction to be studied in rural and remote districts. For conducting an in-depth and insightful study on social media use and addiction, adolescents from developed urban cities—Beijing, Shanghai, Guangzhou, Shenzhen, and Xiamen—were chosen as study sites in this research. These five cities are developed cities in China, with Beijing, Shanghai, and Guangzhou being the three largest cities in China, while Shenzhen and Xiamen are medium-sized cities belonging to two of the special economic zones. Adolescents from these urban centers are considered to have a better quality of life and study environment, as well as international exposure. They have better Internet access both at home and at school and therefore may not only know how to use social media but may also know how to make good use of social media for interpersonal communication. For these reasons adolescents from these five cities were chosen to study social media addiction.

3.2.3 Pilot Tests

Pilot tests of the questionnaire were conducted among 104 adolescents from Shenzhen Shangsha Middle School on December 14, 2010. During the survey, students were encouraged to raise any questions about the questionnaire. After the survey, they were again encouraged to voice any confusion or concerns about the questionnaire—from the wording of the questions to the meaning of the scale. The results of the pilot tests, together with the questions and concerns students raised, helped revise and improve the survey questionnaire before it was finalized.

3.2.4 Sampling Procedure

This survey employed a multistage cluster sampling method. First, five urban cities—Beijing, Shanghai, Guangzhou, Shenzhen, and Xiamen—were chosen in China. Second, middle schools were selected in each of the five cities, with one each from Beijing, Shanghai, and Xiamen and two each from Guangzhou and Shenzhen. Finally, in each selected middle school, one or two classes were randomly chosen in each grade that school has, totaling 45 classes. One day before the survey, a notification was distributed among the students in these randomly selected classes. The notification stated the purpose and significance of the study and asked the parents' permission to allow their sons or daughters to participate in the survey. If the parents refused their sons or daughters to participate, they could sign their name and return the notification to the teachers on the survey day. These students were excused from participating in the survey.

The survey was conducted in classrooms during class time. Some schools allowed the author to enter the classroom to introduce the survey and distribute the questionnaires. At those schools where the author wasn't allowed to do so, teachers read the instructions to participants and administered the questionnaires on behalf of the author. Questionnaires were collected after they were completed. Students participated in the survey voluntarily, and they could refuse to participate. Each student who participated in the survey and finished the questionnaire was awarded a ballpoint pen as a souvenir.

In Beijing, the Affiliated High School of Peking University (北大附中) was chosen. It is a renowned public middle school in Beijing which recruits students from all districts in Beijing every year. It is a typical middle school in Beijing and has a well-equipped computer laboratory that is open to students after class. The Affiliated High School of Peking University had six grades—from Grade 7 to Grade 12. Two classes from each grade were randomly selected; thus students from 12 classes participated. The number of students in each class varied from 45 to 50. A total of 552 questionnaires were distributed in that school. After deleting the invalid questionnaires, the final samples of 425 completed surveys were collected. The response rate was 77.0 %.

In Shanghai, Shanghai Shaoyun Middle School (上海少雲中學) was chosen. It is a typical public high school in Shanghai, which offers Grade 10 to Grade 12. One class of each grade was randomly selected. In these three classes, 146 questionnaires were distributed, and a total of 132 questionnaires were collected after deleting the invalid ones. The response rate was 90.4 %.

In Guangzhou, Guangzhou Qulao Middle School (廣州劬勞中學) and Guangzhou Zhixin High School (廣州執信中學) were selected. Guangzhou Qulao Middle School is a typical public junior middle school in Guangzhou which offers Grade 7 to Grade 9, while Guangzhou Zhixin High School is an important typical public high school in Guangzhou, which has Grade 10 to Grade 12 and recruits students from all districts in Guangzhou. In Qulao Middle School, two classes of each grade from Grade 7 to Grade 9 were randomly selected. In these six selected classes, 276 questionnaires were distributed. After deleting the invalid questionnaires, a total of 205 questionnaires were collected. The response rate was 74.3 %. In Zhixin High School, two classes of each grade from Grade 10 to Grade 12 were randomly selected. A total of 278 questionnaires were distributed in these six classes. After deleting the invalid questionnaires, there were 220 final samples from Guangzhou Zhixin High School. The response rate was 79.1 %.

In Shenzhen, Shenzhen Shangsha Middle School (深圳上沙中學) and Shenzhen Xinzhou Middle School (深圳新洲中學) were chosen. These two schools were both typical public junior middle schools in Shenzhen which offer Grade 7 to Grade 9. One class from each grade was randomly selected in both of these two schools. A total of 138 questionnaires were distributed in three randomly selected classes in Shangsha Middle School, while 146 questionnaires were distributed in three randomly selected classes in Xinzhou Middle School. After deleting the invalid questionnaire, the final samples consisted of 112 and 127 from these two schools. The response rates were 81.2 % and 87.0 %, respectively.

In Xiamen, Xiamen Foreign Language School (廈門外國語中學) was chosen. This school is one of the typical public middle schools in Fujian province, and it recruits students from all over the province every year. There are six grades from Grade 7 to Grade 12. Two classes of each grade were randomly selected; thus 12 classes of students participated. A total of 502 questionnaires were distributed in that school. After deleting the invalid questionnaires, the final samples of Xiamen Foreign Language School were 328. The response rate was 65.3 %.

As a whole, seven middle schools from Beijing, Shanghai, Guangzhou, Shenzhen, and Xiamen participated. A total of 2,038 questionnaires were distributed. The final sample consisted of 1,549 completed surveys and the response rate was 76.0 %. Fieldwork was conducted in these five urban Chinese cities from December 24, 2010, to January 14, 2011. The selected schools comprised both reputable and less reputable schools. As middle schools in China are generally similar in administrative structure and social composition, the population of these seven schools from five cities can be considered representative of adolescents in urban China today.

3.2.5 *Final Sample Profiles*

The sample consisted of 40.5 % boys and 59.5 % girls. However, according to the statistics released by the Ministry of Education of the People's Republic of China (2009), 52.7 % were boys and 47.3 % were girls in junior middle schools in China, while in senior high schools in China, 51.8 % were boys and 48.2 % were girls, and the number doesn't vary much from year to year (MEPRC 2009). Girls were therefore overrepresented in the initial sample. The reason may be that some boys were careless and impatient to finish the questionnaires, while girls tended to be more patient and helpful. To represent the adolescent population in China more accurately, gender was weighted according to the ratio provided by the Ministry of Education of the People's Republic of China. The weighted data were used for all the data analyses that followed.

The final sample still comprised 1,549 cases, but because of the weighting procedure on gender, the number of cases in each city was slightly different from the initial samples. The mean age was 15. The demographics of the final sample are shown in Table 3.1.

3.2.6 *Measures*

3.2.6.1 Level of Social Media Use

Respondents were asked in close-ended questions to indicate their level of use of different kinds of social media, from both the time they spend on that particular medium on average every day to the number of friends they have on that medium. In particular, questions on IM use were: "How long on average do you actively use IM every day (excluding idle time)? How many friends do you have on IM in total? And how many most frequent contact friends do you have on IM?" For SNS use,

Table 3.1 Demographics of the final sample

Characteristics		Frequency	Percentage
Gender	Male	810	52.3
	Female	739	47.7
Age	12	138	8.9
	13	243	15.7
	14	285	18.4
	15	265	17.1
	16	247	16.0
	17	222	14.3
	18	149	9.6
Grade	Grade 7	249	16.1
	Grade 8	373	24.1
	Grade 9	240	15.5
	Grade 10	240	15.5
	Grade 11	244	15.7
	Grade 12	203	13.1
City	Beijing	420	27.1
	Shanghai	141	9.1
	Guangzhou	426	27.5
	Shenzhen	243	15.7
	Xiamen	319	20.6
Total (*N*)		1,549	100

respondents were asked: "How long on average do you use SNS every day? How long on average do you play SNS games every day? How many friends do you have on SNS in total? And how many most frequent contact friends do you have on SNS?" For blog use, questions were: "How long on average do you write blog every day and how long on average do you read others' blog every day?" For microblog use, respondents were asked: "How long on average do you use microblog every day? In microblog, how many followers do you have and how many followings do you have?" When measuring the time, the scale ranged from "do not use," "less than 15 minutes," "15 to 29 minutes," "30 to 59 minutes," "60 to 119 minutes," "120 to 179 minutes," to "180 minutes or more." When measuring the number of friends, the number of frequent contact friends, and the number of followings and followers in microblogs, the scale was "0–10," "11–30," "31–50," "51–100," "101–150," "151–200," and "more than 200."

Cronbach's alpha of the level of use of IM, SNS, blogs, and microblogs were .67, .64, .76, and .84, respectively. It is noticed that since the time the number of friends and the number of most frequent contacted friends were measured on SNS and IM use, the reliabilities were not that high when these items were combined. It might be because some adolescents had many friends on their SNS or IM but did not use them very often or some adolescents used SNS or IM very often but still did not have lots of friends on them. Thus, although the reliability level was not ideally high, these items are still important to include in the measure to indicate the level of

SNS or IM use from different perspectives. In total, Cronbach's alpha for the level of overall social media use combining IM, SNS, blogs, and microblogs was .78.

3.2.6.2 Gratifications

After the focus group, a total of 26 gratification items for social media derived to measure adolescents' social media gratifications-obtained. Respondents were asked to respond on a 5-point Likert-type scale ranging from 1 (strongly disagree) to 5 (strongly agree), with higher scores indicating greater gratifications, to these 26 items about the extent to which social media provided the following gratifications to them:

1. keep in touch with friends whom I can't meet frequently;
2. let friends feel I care about them;
3. understand my friends' recent lives;
4. share my recent life with friends;
5. if I visit my friends' pages frequently, they will visit mine frequently too;
6. if I frequently leave messages or comments on my friends' pages, they will do so on mine;
7. if I share photos or diaries with friends on my page, they will share theirs too;
8. if I give virtual gifts to my friends, they will give to me in return;
9. I can try different online identities;
10. I can hide my real identity online;
11. I can demonstrate identities that are different from daily life;
12. I can demonstrate my ideal self on social media;
13. if I upload messages or photos, my friends will pay attention to them;
14. if I upload messages or photos, my friends will comment on them;
15. if I upload messages or photos, my friends will compliment or support them;
16. if I share my mood with friends on social media, I can get attention and feedback;
17. I can express my thoughts freely on social media;
18. I can express thoughts that I could not express freely in daily life on social media;
19. I can communicate with friends on social media topics that I could not discuss freely face to face;
20. I can gain useful information from social media;
21. I know the current hot topics from social media;
22. I know the topics my friends have paid attention to recently from social media;
23. using social media makes me relax my mood;
24. when I'm upset, talking or communicating with friends on social media makes me feel better;
25. using social media makes me forget bother and trouble; and
26. using social media let me escape from things I should do but do not want to do. A factor analysis generated seven gratification factors that will be discussed in detail in a later analysis.

3.2.6.3 Social Media Addiction

Young's (1996) 20-item Internet Addiction Test was modified to make it suitable for the testing of adolescents' feelings about social media use. The eight items modified from Young's short version of the Internet Addiction Test (Young 1999) were integrated into the final items. Respondents were asked to rank their agreement using a 5-point Likert-type scale ranging from 1 (never) to 5 (all the time). Adolescents' answers to those eight items that had been modified from Young's short version of the Internet Addiction Test were used to identify the adolescents as social media addicts or not, while all the final items were used to measure their level of social media addiction as well as to identify the addiction symptoms. The original eight-item questions were designed as "yes" or "no" questions. According to Young (1999), people were considered "addicted" when answering "yes" to five (or more) of those eight questions. Young (1996) stated that "five" as the cutoff score was consistent with the number of criteria used for pathological gambling and was seen as an adequate number of criteria to differentiate normal from pathologically addictive Internet use. In this research, a 5-point Likert-type scale ranging from 1 (never) to 5 (all the time) was used. In those eight items, respondents who indicated 1 (never) and 2 (seldom) were classified as "no," while those who indicated 3 (sometimes), 4 (often), and 5 (all the time) were classified as "yes." Thus, those who answered five or more questions with "yes" were classified as social media addicts.

The 20-item scale included questions as follows:

1. How often do you find that you use social media longer than you intended?
2. How often do you neglect the things you should do to spend more time on social media?
3. How often do you prefer the excitement of social media to staying with friends?
4. How often do you form new relationships with people on social media?
5. How often do others in your life complain to you about the amount of time you spend on social media?
6. How often do your grades or school work suffer because of the amount of time you spend on social media?
7. How often do you use social media before something else you need to do?
8. How often does your school performance or productivity suffer because of using social media?
9. How often do you become defensive or secretive when anyone asks you what you do on social media?
10. How often do you block out disturbing thoughts about your life with soothing thoughts of the social media?
11. How often do you find yourself anticipating when you will use social media again?
12. How often do you fear that life without the social media would be boring, empty, and joyless?
13. How often do you snap, yell, or act annoyed if someone bothers you while you are using social media?
14. How often do you lose sleep due to late-night log-ins on social media?

15. How often do you feel preoccupied with social media when offline or fantasize about being online?
16. How often do you find yourself saying "just a few more minutes" when using social media?
17. How often do you try to cut down the amount of time you spend on social media but fail?
18. How often do you try to hide for how long you've been using social media?
19. How often do you choose to spend more time on social media instead of going out with others? and
20. How often do you feel depressed, moody, or nervous when you could not use social media, which goes away once you are back online? A factor analysis generated four social media addiction symptoms from this scale, which will be discussed in detail in the later analysis.

In the 20 questions above, Q6, Q8, and Q19 together represent one of the eight questions in Young's eight-item scale (1996); thus the mean of these three questions was calculated to represent that specific question. Seven other items, revised from Young's eight-item scale, were Q1, Q10, Q15, Q16, Q17, Q18, and Q20. It was mentioned above that in these eight items, respondents who indicated 1 (never) and 2 (seldom) were classified as "no," while those who indicated 3 (sometimes), 4 (often) and 5 (all the time) were classified as "yes." Then, adopting Young's classical definition (1996) of Internet addiction, those who indicated five or more questions as "yes" were classified as social media addicts. Cronbach's alpha of this eight-item scale was .79.

3.2.6.4 Need for Affiliation

To assess adolescents' need for affiliation, the Affiliation Motivation Scale designed by Insight Group of Peking University (2002) was used. This is the first scale to measure the need for affiliation of middle-school students in China. The original scale was shortened to be used in this study. Respondents were asked to respond on a 5-point Likert-type scale ranging from 1 (strongly disagree) to 5 (strongly agree) to five questions concerning their need for affiliation. The items were (1) I usually make as many friends as possible; (2) I would like to stay with friends and know more about them; (3) I would like to join warm and friendly groups; (4) I care about my friends; and (5) I think any experience will become meaningful if I share it with friends. Cronbach's alpha of this five-item scale was .87. The total score of these five items were used to represent adolescents' need for affiliation, with the higher the score, the more the adolescents' need for affiliation.

3.2.6.5 Impression Management

The modified Self-Presentation Tactics Scale (Lee et al. 1999) was used. Self-presentation tactics are behaviors for impression management to achieve

Table 3.2 Factor analysis of narcissism personality of adolescents

	Mean	SD	Factor 1	2	3	4
Exploitativeness						
1. It is easy for me to control other people	2.87	.97	.81			
2. I can make people believe anything I want them to	3.14	.98	.76			
3. I'm good at getting people to do things my way	3.01	.96	.74			
Leadership						
4. It matters whether I am the leader or not	3.34	1.09		.84		
5. I like to be in charge of other people	2.96	1.06		.77		
6. I like to be the center of attention	3.05	1.09		.76		
Self-absorption						
7. I like it when others brag about the good things I have done	3.45	1.07			.89	
8. I like it when people tell me I have done a good job	3.50	1.08			.87	
9. I like to look at myself in the mirror a lot	2.75	1.19			.57	
Superiority						
10. I'm going to be a great person	3.12	1.08				.77
11. I'm really a special person	3.66	1.03				.74
12. I was born a good leader	2.94	1.08				.61
Eigenvalues			4.45	1.70	1.42	.85
Variance explained (%)			19.86	17.94	16.62	15.69
Cronbach's alpha			.82	.74	.72	.76

Note: Scale: 1 = not at all like me and 5 = completely like me. Total variance, 70.12 %. N = 1,541

interpersonal goals (Lee et al. 1999). This scale was used to assess various tactics associated with impression management. Rosenberg (2009) modified it to measure individuals' impression management on Facebook. Again, the scale was modified in this study to make it suitable for the measuring of Chinese adolescents' competence of impression management tactics on social media. The respondents were asked to respond on a 5-point Likert-type scale ranging from 1 (very infrequently) to 5 (very frequently) to 12 items as follows:

1. I share my good scores or positive accomplishments with friends in social media;
2. I share my daily or travel photos on which I look good with friends in social media;
3. I make my friends know my strengths through social media;
4. I praise my friends in social media so that they will see me as friendly;
5. I compliment the experiences of my friends in social media so that they are willing to share their experiences with me;
6. I pay attention to my friends in social media so that they would think I care about them;

7. When I'm blamed for something, I make excuses on social media;
8. When I do not get a good grade, I explain in social media that it is not all my fault;
9. I depreciate my rival on social media;
10. If I have done something wrong, I will apologize to my friends through social media;
11. If I hurt my friends, I will apologize to them through social media; and
12. I offer explanations or justify my behavior for negative events in social media to reduce the negative impression others have of me. A factor analysis yielded four impression management tactics in social media for adolescents, which will be discussed in detail in a later analysis.

3.2.6.6 Narcissism

The revised Narcissism Personality Questionnaire for Children (Ang and Yusof 2006) was used to measure adolescents' narcissism. It was revised and shortened to be suitable for Chinese adolescents. Respondents were asked to respond, using a 5-point Likert-type scale ranging from 1 (not at all like me) to 5 (completely like me), to 12 items that assessed their narcissism personality.

For narcissism among Chinese adolescents, as shown in Table 3.2 and in line with the previous literature, a factor analysis generated four dimensions of the adolescent narcissism personality, explaining 70.12 % of the total variance. The first factor was "exploitativeness" ($\alpha = .82$; eigenvalue = 4.45; 19.86 % of the variance explained), which consisted of three items characterizing that adolescents thought they could control others easily, made others believe anything, and got others to do things their way. "Leadership" was the second factor ($\alpha = .74$; eigenvalue = 1.70; 17.94 % of the variance explained). It consisted of three items illustrating that adolescents did not mind whether they were the leader in a group or not and did not like to be in charge of other people and be the center of attention. These three items were reverse-coded. "Self-absorption" was the third factor ($\alpha = .72$; eigenvalue = 1.42; 16.62 % of the variance explained). It contained three items reflecting that adolescents liked others bragging about the good things they had done and praising them and they liked looking at themselves in the mirror a lot. The fourth factor, superiority ($\alpha = .76$; eigenvalue = .85; 15.69 % of the variance explained) contained three items indicating that adolescents thought they were born to be good leaders, were really special persons, or were going to be great persons. These four dimensions constructed adolescents' narcissism personality. The factor loading of each factor is shown in Table 3.2.

3.2.6.7 Leisure Boredom

To assess perceptions of boredom in leisure, a modified Leisure Boredom Scale (Iso-Ahola and Weissinger 1990) was used. The authors suggested that the original

Table 3.3 Factor analysis of adolescents' social capital

			Factor	
	Mean	SD	1	2
Bonding social capital				
1. There is someone I can turn to for advice when making very important decisions	3.91	.90	.81	
2. There are several people I trust to help me solve my problems	3.87	.95	.80	
3. There is someone I feel comfortable talking to about intimate personal problems	3.87	1.03	.78	
4. I know people well enough to get them to do something important	4.06	.90	.73	
5. When I feel lonely, there are several people I can talk to	3.85	1.02	.72	
Bridging social capital				
6. Interacting with people makes me want to try new things	3.78	.92		.84
7. Interacting with people makes me interested in what people unlike me are thinking	3.94	.87		.79
8. Interacting with people makes me interested in things that happen outside	3.87	.87		.79
9. Interacting with people makes me feel part of a larger community	3.92	.91		.72
10. Interacting with people gives me new people to talk to	3.86	.92		.69
Eigenvalues			5.42	1.25
Variance explained (%)			33.39	33.29
Cronbach's alpha			.87	.87

Note: Scale: 1 = not at all like me and 5 = completely like me. Total variance, 66.68 %. N = 1,545

scale was potentially usable in clinical and applied research involving diagnosing leisure dysfunctions such as substance abuse (Iso-Ahola and Weissinger 1990). The original Leisure Boredom Scale was shortened and modified to make it suitable for Chinese adolescents. The scale contained 5 items asking adolescents to indicate how they felt about their leisure time. Respondents were asked to respond on a 5-point Likert-type scale ranging from 1 (strongly disagree) to 5 (strongly agree) to the following five items: (1) my leisure time is boring; (2) I usually do not know what to do in my leisure time; (3) I waste too much of my leisure time sleeping; (4) I'm not active during my leisure time; and (5) leisure time activities do not excite me. Cronbach's alpha of this five-item scale was .81. The total score of these five items was used to represent adolescents' level of leisure boredom, with higher scores indicating greater leisure boredom.

3.2.6.8 Academic Performance

Respondents were asked to indicate their scores of the latest formal big examination (such as midterm or term examination) and the latest tests scores in Chinese, Mathematics, and English. A 5-point Likert-type scale was used, through 1 = "60 and below," 2="60–69," 3="70–79," 4="80–89," and 5="90–100," with 100 as the full mark. Cronbach's alpha of these items was .85. The scores were standardized to make it comparable. The standardized total scores were used to represent adolescents' academic performance, with the higher the scores, the better the academic performance.

3.2.6.9 Social Capital

The Social Capital Scale by Williams (2006) was revised and used to measure the social capital of Chinese adolescents. This scale was designed to measure both the offline and online social capital people had. Respondents were asked to respond on a 5-point Likert-type scale ranging from 1 (strongly disagree) to 5 (strongly agree) to 10 items, with high scores indicating greater social capital.

As shown in Table 3.3, a principal component factor analysis generated two dimensions for adolescents' social capital, which accounts for 66.68 % of the total variance. The first dimension was "bonding social capital" ($\alpha = .87$; eigenvalue = 5.42; 33.39 % of the variance explained), which consisted of five items reflecting social capital arising from strong and intimate ties: there were persons one could turn to for advice on important decisions or for helping solve problems; there were persons one could feel comfortable to talk to or ask for help with something important. The second dimension was "bridging social capital" ($\alpha = .87$; eigenvalue = 1.25; 33.29 % of the variance explained). It included five items characterizing that adolescents thought interacting with others made them want to try new things, meet new friends to talk to, and make them feel members of a large community. They were interested in things happening outside and would like to know other people's thoughts. Bonding and bridging social capital are two dimensions constructing adolescents' social capital, which are in accordance with the previous literature. The factor loading is shown in Table 3.3.

3.2.6.10 Parental Control

Parental control was measured in three items on a 5-point Likert-type scale ranging from 1 (never) to 5 (always), asking adolescents how often parents (1) limit their online time, (2) limit the website they browse, and (3) pay attention to whom they interact with online. Cronbach's alpha of these three items was .71. The total score of these three items were used to represent parental control of adolescents' online behavior, with higher scores indicating greater parental mediation.

3.2.6.11 Overall Internet Use

To provide an overall understanding of adolescents' Internet behavior, some questions concerning adolescents' general Internet use were also asked.

When answering "which do you use to get online most frequently, a computer or mobile phone?" 80 % of the respondents indicated that they used a computer to get online more frequently, while the other 20 % indicated that they used a mobile phone. During the focus group sessions, some adolescents indeed showed the author how they used mobile QQ or updated their microblogs by means of a mobile phone. They told the author that they often secretly used a mobile phone to connect to social media at school after class, at home when doing homework in their rooms, or on the bus.

When answering where they got online most frequently, nearly 60 % of the respondents indicated "at home in an open-door room," while about 20 % of them chose "at home in a closed-door room"; 14 % of them said "at home in the living room," 4 % were "at school," only 2 % were "in an Internet café," and 0.6 % were "in a friend's home." More than half of the respondents got online in the open-door room at home, which indicates that many parents indeed maintain certain monitoring or control over adolescents' behaviors. Although adolescents who are under 18 years old are forbidden to enter an Internet café in China, there were still some adolescents who got online there.

Respondents were asked for how long on average they used the Internet every day. Among the respondents, 98.4 % used the Internet. For average everyday use, 44 % of the respondents used the Internet for less than 1 h, while the remaining 56 % used the Internet for more than 1 h a day, and more than 10 % of the respondents even got online for more than 4 h a day. The category mean was 3.93, which revealed that, on average, adolescents spent about 1 h on the Internet every day. In focus groups, some adolescents said that they used a computer to do their homework every day, and some courses had online exercise modules. Although not sufficient, long hours online every day indicates that some adolescents were indeed addicted to the Internet.

Respondents were also asked about their years of online experience. The data showed that students began to use the Internet when they were very young. Approximately 90 % of the respondents had used Internet for more than 3 years, and 15 % of them had even used it for more than 8 years. The category mean was 3.94, which suggested that the respondents on average had used the Internet for 4 years. These data indicate that the Internet has penetrated people's lives since they were very young.

3.2.6.12 Demographics

Basic demographic information was also asked, such as gender, age, grade in school, monthly family income, parental marital status, and the city in which they live.

3.2.7 Analytical Procedure

The study adopted various kinds of bivariate and multivariate statistical analyses to test the hypotheses and answer the research questions. Correlation analyses were conducted to test all the hypotheses. Frequency tests were used to generate descriptive data to answer RQ_1 about the level of social media use among adolescents in urban China. To solve RQ_2, RQ_4, and RQ_5, a factor analysis was conducted to yield seven gratifications adolescents obtained from social media use, four social media addiction symptoms adolescents experienced, and four impression management tactics adolescents used in social media. Factor analyses were also used to generate four narcissism dimensions and two social capital dimensions for adolescents. Reliability analyses were undertaken to ensure the reliability of scales and factors.

To answer RQ_3 about the profile of social-media-addicted adolescents and to answer RQ_8 to identify the factors that could discriminate between social media addicts and nonaddicts, the t test and a discriminant analysis were used, respectively.

Hierarchical regression analyses were conducted to solve RQ_6, RQ_7, and RQ_9 to establish the significant predictors for social media gratifications, social media use, and social media addiction. Hierarchical regressions were also used to identify the powerful predictors for adolescents' academic performance and social capital, which helped to answer RQ_{10} and RQ_{11}. A series of regression tests were also conducted to examine the mediation effects suggested by the findings.

3.3 Focus Groups

Before the survey, focus groups among adolescents were organized. Thirty adolescents from Xiamen Foreign Language School were recruited to participate voluntarily. Twelve of them were from junior grades (Grades 7–9) and 18 of them were from senior grades (Grades 10–12). They were divided into four groups. The focus group sessions were conducted on November 15–16, 2010, during the extracurricular activity time in the afternoon in one conference room at Xiamen Foreign Language School. Each session lasted about 1 h.

The author first introduced what the social media are to the participants. The social media topic soon attracted students' interest. They talked actively during the focus groups and even debated with each other. Originally, the author did not expect microblogs to be popular among adolescents. During the focus groups, some students emphasized that they now used microblogs a lot and showed the author how they updated microblogs by their mobile phones. They asked the author to keep secrets as the school did not allow them to use mobile phones at school.

During the focus group sessions, the following topics were discussed: the popular social media among adolescents and their general usage pattern; when, where, and how frequently they used social media; the social and psychological origins of their social media use; the gratifications they obtained from social media and the purpose for which they constantly used social media; what impression management tactics they adopted; whether some of them or their friends were addicted to social media and the possible symptoms they observe; the positive and negative consequences of their social media use and addiction; and parents' or teachers' control of their social media use.

Students were very active in the focus group discussions. The data gained from focus groups were used to finalize the research design and variables to be tested in the survey. The focus group data were also used to construct social media gratification items, modify some other exiting scales, as well as name factors indicating social media gratifications and addiction symptoms.

3.4 In-Depth Interviews

To provide an overall picture of adolescents' social media addiction, after the survey data analysis, 15 parents and 15 teachers of those adolescents who participated in the survey were invited to one-to-one in-depth interviews. To gather more integrated information, some of those parents had sons and others had daughters, and their sons or daughters were in various grades. Most of the teachers were in charge of the classes; thus they were more familiar with students' daily behaviors and were responsible for keeping in touch with the parents.

The interviews started with a carefully designed outline, but the outline was adjusted during the interview process according to the reaction or answers obtained from different parents and teachers. They were therefore semi-structured interviews. Generally, the topics covered during the interviews with the parents were the following: the social media use of their children; whether their children were addicted to social media or had some misuse behaviors; the parents' attitudes toward their children's social media use; whether and how they controlled their children's social media use and Internet behavior and the effects; and, in their opinion, the impact of social media on their children's academic performance and social capital. When interviewing teachers, the topics included the status of social media use among students in their class; whether some students were addicted to social media or had some misuse behaviors, and the profiles of those students; as teachers, their attitudes toward students' social media use; whether and how they controlled students' social media use and the effects; whether schools had some regulations concerning students' social media use; and the possible impact of social media on students' academic performance and social capital.

Each interview lasted from 30 min to 1 h. Most parents and teachers were active, sharing their concerns and worries about adolescents' social media addiction.

References

Ang, R., & Yusof, N. (2006). Development and initial validation of the narcissistic personality questionnaire for children: A preliminary investigation using school-based Asian samples. *Educational Psychology, 26*(1), 1–18.

Encyclopedia of Children's Health. (2011). *Adolescence*. Retrieved May 13, 2011, from http://www.healthofchildren.com/A/Adolescence.html

Erikson, E. H. (1950). *Childhood and society*. New York: W. W. Norton.

Haffner, D. (1995). *Facing facts: Sexual health for America's adolescents*. New York: SIECUS.
Insight Group. (2002). Affiliation motivation scale. *Psychological Test Tool Box for Middle School V2.0.* Peking University.
Iso-Ahola, S. E., & Weissinger, E. (1990). Perceptions of boredom in leisure: Conceptualization, reliability and validity of the leisure boredom scale. *Journal of Leisure Research, 22*(1), 1–17.
Lee, S., Quigley, B. M., Nesler, M. S., Corbett, A. B., & Tedeschi, J. T. (1999). Development of a self-presentation tactics scale. *Personality and Individual Differences, 26*, 701–722.
Marcell, A. V. (2007). Adolescence. In R. M. Kliegman, R. E. Behrman, H. B. Jenson, & B. F. Stanton (Eds.), *Nelson textbook of pediatrics* (18th ed., pp. 60–64). Philadelphia: Saunders Elsevier.
Ministry of Education of the People's Republic of China (MEPRC). (2009). *2009 Education statistics.* Retrieved April 10, 2011, from http://www.moe.edu.cn/publicfiles/business/htmlfiles/moe/s4958/list.html
Rosenberg, J. (2009). *Online impression management: Personality traits and concern for secondary goals as predictors of self-presentation tactics on Facebook.* Unpublished master's thesis. Kent State University, Kent, OH, USA.
Violato, C., & Travis, L. D. (1995). *Advances in adolescent psychology*. Calgary: Detselig Enterprises.
Williams, D. (2006). On and off the net: Scales for social capital in an online era. *Journal of Computer-Mediated Communication, 11*, 593–628.
Young, K. S. (1996). *Caught in the net: How to recognize the signs of Internet addiction—and a winning strategy for recovery*. New York: Wiley.
Young, K. S. (1999). Internet addiction: Symptoms, evaluation, and treatment. In L. VandeCreek & T. Jackson (Eds.), *Innovations in clinical practice: A source book* (Vol. 17, pp. 19–31). Sarasota: Professional Resource Press.

Chapter 4
Uses, Gratifications, and Addiction of Social Media

This chapter discusses social media addiction among adolescents in urban China from the U&G perspectives. Specifically, it covers social media penetration among adolescents in urban China, the gratifications adolescents obtained from social media use, the severity of social media addiction among adolescents in urban China, and social media addiction symptoms the adolescents experience. Moreover, the chapter elaborates on the relationships of social media addiction relative to the level of social media use, gratifications, and parental control.

4.1 Social Media Penetrations Among Adolescents in Urban China

RQ_1 asked the degree to which adolescents in urban China use social media including IM, SNS, blogs, and microblogs. To answer this research question, adolescents were asked to indicate their level of use of IM, SNS, blogs, and microblogs in terms of the time spent daily on each medium on average and the number of friends they had on a specific medium. Tables 4.1 and 4.2 show the frequency of use and the number of friends the adolescents had on each social medium, respectively.

IM indeed ranked as the most popular social medium among adolescents, with 90 % of the respondents reporting that they were IM users. The survey questionnaire emphasized that the usage time meant the active use time, which excluded idle time when IM applications remained in the background and not in active use. Nearly 30 % of the respondents indicated that they used IM more than 1 h every day, and 10.4 % reported using it more than 3 h a day. These data reflect heavy use of IM by some of the adolescents. As for the total number of friends on IM, 45 % of the respondents reported more than 100 friends on IM. However, 90 % of the respondents had fewer than 50 frequent contact friends on IM. This indicates that while adolescents may have a large number of casual IM friends, they may often limit IM communication to certain intimate friends. The category means for daily IM use,

H. Huang, *Social Media Generation in Urban China: A Study of Social Media Use and Addiction among Adolescents*, Understanding China,
DOI 10.1007/978-3-642-45441-7_4, © Springer-Verlag Berlin Heidelberg 2014

Table 4.1 Frequency of daily social media use

		SNS		Blogs		
Daily use	IM (%)	Overall (%)	Game (%)	Writing (%)	Reading (%)	Microblogs (%)
Users	90.0	51.3	48.2	44.4	65.6	40.4
1. No use	10.0	48.7	51.8	55.6	34.4	59.6
2. < than 15 min	24.5	20.5	27.3	23.2	31.5	17.9
3. 15–29 min	17.8	13.8	12.1	10.6	19.1	10.1
4. 30–59 min	18.0	8.3	5.8	7.4	10.2	6.3
5. 60–119 min	13.6	5.3	1.3	2.3	3.5	3.5
6. 120–179 min	5.5	1.3	0.5	0.4	0.8	1.0
7. ≧180 min	10.4	2.0	1.2	0.5	0.5	1.5
Category Mean	3.59	2.13	1.84	1.81	2.21	1.85

Note: N = 1,549

Table 4.2 Number of friends on social media

	IM		SNS		Microblogs	
	Total friends (%)	Frequent contact friends (%)	Total friends (%)	Frequent contact friends (%)	Followers (%)	Followings (%)
1. 0–10	9.8	42.0	52.9	70.2	69.2	66.5
2. 11–30	9.6	36.4	10.1	18.8	12.0	14.6
3. 31–50	14.3	12.5	8.9	7.3	5.9	8.0
4. 51–100	21.4	6.7	9.9	2.5	6.1	5.8
5. 101–150	16.3	1.0	5.7	0.7	3.0	2.0
6. 151–200	10.5	1.0	3.4	0.3	0.7	1.1
7. > 200	18.0	0.4	9.2	0.3	3.1	1.9
Category Mean	4.28	1.93	2.52	1.47	1.76	1.73

Note: N = 1,549

total IM friends, and frequent contact IM friends were 3.59, 4.28, and 1.93, respectively. This suggests that, on average, the adolescents spent 30–59 min engaged in IM everyday; they had more than 100 but fewer than 150 total IM friends on average but only 11–30 frequent-contact IM friends.

Data also indicate 51.3 % and 48.2 % of the respondents as users of SNS and SNS games, respectively. Nearly 10 % of the respondents used SNS more than 1 h every day. SNS games had great popularity in 2009 and 2010 at their introduction, but their popularity has waned as of this research. Less than 10 % of the respondents spent more than 30 min playing SNS games daily. As for the total number of friends on SNS, nearly 20 % of the respondents had more than 100 friends on SNS, but around 90 % of them had fewer than 30 frequent contact friends on SNS. These data indicate that adolescents may connect with each other through SNS for information sharing or other online activities, but we might consider most of these connections as weak. Only some of the connections are strong enough to provide emotional support for them. The category means for SNS use, SNS game use, total friends on SNS, and frequent contact friends on SNS were 2.13, 1.84, 2.52, and 1.47, respectively. This reveals that, on average, adolescents daily used SNS for 15–30 min and spent fewer than 15 min playing SNS games; they had more than 30 but fewer than 50 friends on SNS on average, and more than 11 but fewer than 30 frequent contact friends on SNS.

As for blogs, more than 65 % of the respondents read others' blogs, while 44.4 % of the respondents wrote and maintained their own personal blogs. Over 10 % and 15 % of the respondents spent longer than half an hour writing their own blogs and reading others' blogs, respectively. The category means for blog writing and blog reading were 1.81 and 2.21, respectively. This indicates that, on average, adolescents spent 15–30 min reading others' blogs but spent fewer than 15 min writing and maintaining their own blogs daily.

Of the participants, 40.4 % use microblogs, and over 12 % of the respondents spent more than half an hour a day on microblogs. Around 20 % of them followed more than 30 microblogs. Interestingly, 13 % of the respondents had more than 50 followers in their microblogs. These data indicate an increasing popularity of microblogs among adolescents. The category mean for microblog use, number of followers, and number of followings were 1.85, 1.76, and 1.73, respectively. This suggests that on average, the adolescents spent fewer than 15 min on microblogs daily, and they had between 11 and 30 both followers and followings.

4.2 Adolescent Gratifications-Obtained from Social Media

RQ_2 asked about the gratifications adolescents obtained from social media use. To answer this research question, principal component factor analysis was conducted to generate seven gratifications-obtained dimensions for adolescent social media use, explaining 68.78 % of the total variance. The original 26 items were constructed from focus group interviews. Table 4.3 shows the first factor, "peer attention" (α=.90; eigenvalue=7.89; 11.80 % of the variance explained), consisting of four items reflecting that adolescents could attract and obtain peer attention by social media activities. If they uploaded messages or photos on social media, their friends might reply with comments, compliments, or support and generally pay attention to them; if they shared moods with friends on social media, they might receive attention and feedback. "Social exchange," the second factor (α=.83; eigenvalue=2.37; explained 11.13 % of the variance), included four items emphasizing reciprocity among users of social media. For example, if a social media user visited friends' pages and posted messages or commented frequently, the friends might reciprocate; if a social media user shared photos or diaries with friends, the friends might share theirs in return; and if a social media user gave virtual gifts to friends, the friends might return the favor. "Friendship maintenance," the third factor (α=.80; eigenvalue=1.96; explained 10.92 % of the variance), consisted of four items illustrating that social media helped adolescents to maintain friendships. Social media users can follow friends' lives, keep in touch with those they do not see frequently, and let

Table 4.3 Factor analysis of social media gratifications among adolescents

			Factor						
	Mean	SD	1	2	3	4	5	6	7
Peer attention									
1. If I upload messages or photos, my friends will comment on them	3.54	.88	.86						
2. If I upload messages or photos, my friends will compliment or support them	3.40	.89	.81						
3. If I upload messages or photos, my friends will pay attention to them	3.55	.90	.79						
4. If I share mood with friends on social media, I can get attention and feedback	3.63	.90	.67						
Social exchange									
5. If I frequently leave messages or comments on my friends' pages, they will do so on mine	3.40	.97		.82					
6. If I share photos or diaries with friends on my page, they will share theirs too	3.27	.97		.77					
7. If I visit my friends' page frequently, they will visit mine frequently too	3.34	.98		.76					
8. If I give virtual gifts to my friends, they will give to me in return	3.39	1.01		.66					
Friendship maintenance									
9. Understand my friends' recent lives	3.70	.91			.81				
10. Share my recent life with friends	3.65	.94			.75				
11. Let friends feel I care about them	3.53	.90			.70				
12. Keep in touch with friends who you can't meet frequently	3.71	1.00			.69				
Information seeking									
13. I can know the current hot topics from social media	4.01	.92				.88			
14. I can gain useful information from social media	4.00	.91				.81			
15. I can know the topics my friends paid attention to recently from social media	3.89	.92				.80			

(continued)

Table 4.3 (continued)

	Mean	SD	Factor 1	2	3	4	5	6	7
Identity creation and management									
16. I can hide my real identity online	3.44	1.13					.80		
17. I can demonstrate identities that are different from daily life	3.32	1.10					.78		
18. I can try different online identities	2.97	1.17					.75		
19. I can demonstrate my ideal-self on social media	3.35	1.04					.65		
Free expression									
20. I can express thoughts that I could not express freely in daily life on social media	3.66	1.03						.82	
21. I can express my thoughts freely on social media	3.81	.92						.76	
22. I can communicate with friends on social media topics that I could not discuss freely face to face	3.58	1.05						.55	
Escape									
23. Using social media makes me forget bother and trouble	3.12	1.04							.84
24. Using social media let me escape things that I should do but I don't want to do	2.60	1.13							.78
25. When I'm upset, talking or communicating with friends on social media makes me feel better	3.71	.99							.59
Eigenvalues			7.89	2.37	1.96	1.46	1.31	1.19	1.02
Variance explained (%)			11.80	11.13	10.92	9.73	9.64	7.98	7.58
Cronbach's alpha			.90	.83	.80	.87	.77	.73	.71

Note: Scale: 1 = Strongly disagree and 5 = Strongly agree. Total variance: 68.78 %. N = 1,523

friends know they care enough to stay in touch. The fourth factor, "information seeking" (α = .87; eigenvalue = 1.46; explained 9.73 % of the variance), contained three items relating to adolescents obtaining information from social media. Social media users can learn from topical issues, know what friends are paying attention to, and gain useful information. "Identity creation and management," the fifth factor (α = .77; eigenvalue = 1.31; explained 9.64 % of the variance), consisted of four items. These characterized adolescents' hiding their real identities online, trying on different online identities, creating ideal-selves, and otherwise assuming new and different identities. The sixth factor, "free expression" (α=.73; eigenvalue=1.19; 7.98 % of the variance explained), consisted of three items illustrating adolescents' expressing their thoughts freely on social media. Using social media, they felt they could express thoughts that they could not express freely in daily life or they felt they could communicate with friends on social media topics that could not be discussed freely face to face. "Escape," the last factor (α=.71; eigenvalue=1.02; 7.58 % of the variance explained), contained three items reflecting how social media made some adolescents forget their troubles in daily life and escape from things that they should do but did not want to do. When upset, talking or communicating with friends on social media made them feel better.

These seven gratifications can be further categorized according to their functions. In particular, "friendship maintenance," "social exchange," and "peer attention" can be categorized as fulfilling "social gratifications"; "free expression" and "information seeking" can be considered "information gratifications"; and "identity creation and management" and "escape" can be seen as serving "entertainment gratifications." "Social gratifications" are unique for social media; they emphasize the "social" features of social media.

4.3 Severity of Social Media Addiction Among Adolescents

RQ_3 asked about the degree of social media addiction of adolescents in urban China and who these social media addicts are. Using the classic definition of Internet addiction by Young (1999) discussed earlier, 15.6 % of the adolescents in this sample could be classified as social media addicts. Independent sample T-tests were performed to examine possible differences between addicts and nonaddicts in terms of the level of use of each social medium. By calculating from category means, on average, social media addicts spent around 3 h daily on social media; nonaddicts spent approximately 110 min on average everyday on social media.

As Table 4.4 illustrates, social media addicts indeed used social media more everyday and had more total friends and more frequent contact friends on social media than nonaddicts. Regarding IM use, compared to nonaddicts, social media addicts used IM more everyday (M=4.42, SD=1.90 vs. M=3.43, SD=1.72; t=−7.50, p<.001), had more total friends (M=4.85, SD=1.78 vs. M=4.18, SD=1.88; t=−5.07, p<.001), and more frequent contact friends (M=2.33, SD=1.28 vs. M=1.85, SD=1.00; t=−5.50, p<.001) on IM. The addicts used both SNS (M=2.48, SD=1.61 vs. M=2.05, SD=1.42; t=−3.82, p<.001) and SNS games (M=2.10, SD=1.41 vs. M=1.78, SD=1.10; t=−3.29, p<.001) more every day, had more total friends (M=3.02, SD=2.07 vs. M=2.42, SD=2.00; t=−4.28, p<.001), and more frequent contact friends (M=1.64, SD=.98 vs. M=1.43, SD=.85; t=−3.12, p<.01) on SNS than nonaddicts. Social media addicted adolescents also spent more time than nonaddicts reading blogs (M=2.52, SD=1.25 vs. M=2.15, SD=1.19; t=−4.25, p<.001), writing blogs (M=2.02, SD=1.35 vs. M=1.76, SD=1.10; t=−2.75, p<.01), and updating microblogs (M=2.11, SD=1.50 vs. M=1.79, SD=1.29; t=−3.05, p<.01). They had more followers (M=2.13, SD=1.73 vs. M=1.68. SD=1.37; t=−3.87, p<.001) and

Table 4.4 Means and standard deviation of level of social media use for social media addicts and nonaddicts

	Addicts		Nonaddicts		
Variable	*M*	SD	*M*	SD	*t*
Daily use					
IM	4.42	1.90	3.43	1.72	−7.50***
SNS	2.48	1.61	2.05	1.42	−3.82***
SNS game	2.10	1.41	1.78	1.10	−3.29***
Blog writing	2.02	1.35	1.76	1.10	−2.75**
Blog reading	2.52	1.25	2.15	1.19	−4.25***
Microblogs	2.11	1.50	1.79	1.29	−3.05**
Total friends on IM	4.85	1.78	4.18	1.88	−5.07***
Frequent contact friends on IM	2.33	1.28	1.85	1.00	−5.50***
Total friends on SNS	3.02	2.07	2.42	2.00	−4.28***
Frequent contact friends on SNS	1.64	.98	1.43	.85	−3.12**
Followings on microblogs	2.08	1.64	1.65	1.24	−3.84***
Followers on microblogs	2.13	1.73	1.68	1.37	−3.87***
Daily Internet use	4.46	1.72	3.83	1.52	−5.28***
Years of online experience	4.05	1.22	3.92	1.27	−1.52 n.s.

Note: ***$p<.001$; **$p<.01$. $N=1{,}529$–$1{,}532$

more followings ($M=2.08$, SD = 1.64 vs. $M=1.65$, SD = 1.24; $t=-3.84$, $p<.001$) than nonaddicts had in their microblogs. Addicts also spent more time on the Internet everyday than nonaddicts did ($M=4.46$, SD = 1.72 vs. $M=3.83$, SD = 1.52; $t=-5.28$, $p<.001$). However, results showed no significant difference between social media addicts and nonaddicts in terms of their years of online experience ($M=4.05$, SD = 1.22 vs. $M=3.92$, SD = 1.27; $t=-1.52$, n.s.).

4.4 Social Media Addiction Symptoms Among Adolescents

RQ_4 attempted to identify social media addiction symptoms among adolescents in urban China. To answer this question, the social media addiction scale, modified from Young's (1996) 20-item Internet Addiction Test, was used to identify social media addiction symptoms. As shown in Table 4.5, principal component factor analysis generated a four-factor social media addiction structure and accounted for 60.15 % of total variance. The first factor, "preoccupation" ($\alpha=.79$; eigenvalue = 5.70; explained 18.15 % of the variance), consisted of six items on adolescents preoccupied by social media. The adolescents felt preoccupied with social media when offline and fantasized about being online: they often said "just a few more minutes," to themselves when using social media; they tried but failed to cut down on the amount of time spent on social media; they hid the time they spent on social media; they felt depressed, moody, or nervous when they could not use social media; and/or they snapped, yelled, or acted annoyed if someone bothered them when they were using social media. "Adverse consequences" was the second factor

Table 4.5 Factor analysis of social media addiction symptoms among adolescents

			Factor			
	Mean	SD	1	2	3	4
Preoccupation						
1. How often do you feel preoccupied with social media when offline or fantasize about being online?	1.94	1.02	.65			
2. How often do you find yourself saying "just a few more minutes" when using social media?	1.97	1.05	.63			
3. How often do you try to cut down the amount of time you spend on social media but fail?	1.68	.90	.61			
4. How often do you try to hide how long you've been using social media?	1.69	.94	.60			
5. How often do you feel depressed, moody, or nervous when you could not use social media, which goes away once you are back online?	1.49	.84	.60			
6. How often do you snap, yell, or act annoyed if someone bothers you while you are using social media?	1.82	.95	.54			
Adverse consequences						
7. How often do your grades or school work suffers because of the amount of time you spend on social media?	2.12	.99		.80		
8. How often do you use social media before something else that you need to do?	2.02	.92		.70		
9. How often does your school performance or productivity suffer because of using social media?	1.75	.86		.68		
10. How often do you neglect the things you should do to spend more time on social media?	2.33	.99		.63		
Alleviation of negative emotions						
11. How often do you block out disturbing thoughts about your life or bad mood by communicating with friends in social media?	2.79	1.27			.78	
12. How often do you find yourself anticipating when you will use social media again?	2.58	1.10			.73	
13. How often do you feel that life without the social media is boring, empty, and joyless?	2.15	1.10			.55	

(continued)

Table 4.5 (continued)

	Mean	SD	Factor 1	2	3	4
Loss of interest in social activities						
14. How often do you choose to spend more time on social media over going out with others?	1.62	.89				.81
15. How often do you prefer the excitement of social media to staying with friends?	1.85	.93				.78
Eigenvalues			5.70	1.31	1.13	.89
Variance explained (%)			18.15	16.36	14.90	10.74
Cronbach's alpha			.79	.78	.68	.65

Note: Scale: 1 = Not at all and 5 = Always. Total variance: 60.15 %. N = 1,528

(α = .78; eigenvalue = 1.31; explained 16.36 % of the variance). It contained four items reflecting the negative consequences adolescents might suffer from social media addiction. Their grades and academic performance and productivity might suffer because of overuse of social media; they turned to social media before other required tasks and neglected things they should do to spend more time on social media. "Alleviation of negative emotion," the third factor (α = .68; eigenvalue = 1.13; explained 14.90 % of the variance), included three items illustrating how adolescents used social media to alleviate negative emotions. They blocked out disturbing thoughts about their lives or bad moods by communicating with friends through social media; they considered life without social media boring, empty, and joyless; and they found that they anticipated social media use. The fourth factor, "loss of interest in social activities" (α = .65; eigenvalue = .89; explained 10.74 % of the variance), contained two items relating to adolescents' choosing to spend more time on social media over socializing with friends offline and preferring the excitement of social media over actual interactions with friends. Table 4.5 shows the factor loading. These four factors demonstrate the symptoms social media addicts might experience.

A composite social media addiction index was created by combining these 15 items with Cronbach's alpha equals to .88, which represented the overall level of adolescent social media addiction.

4.5 Linking Gratifications-Obtained to Level of Social Media Use

H_1 proposed that the more the adolescents in urban China find social media gratifying, the more they will use social media. As expected, bivariate correlation results in Table 4.6 show all seven gratifications from social media significantly and positively correlated with each kind of social medium use (r ranged from .05 to .26). Therefore, H_1 was supported.

Table 4.6 Summary of the correlation results between gratifications-obtained and level of social media use

Variable	IM	SNS	Blog	Microblogs
Friendship maintenance	.20***	.20***	.21***	.16***
Social exchange	.26***	.22***	.21***	.11***
Peer attention	.24***	.22***	.22***	.17***
Free expression	.22***	.06*	.16***	.14***
Information seeking	.11***	.11***	.14***	.17***
Identity creation and management	.15***	.05*	.12***	.07**
Escape	.26***	.14***	.15***	.14***

Note: $^{*}p<.05$; $^{**}p<.01$; $^{***}p<.001$. $N=1{,}532$–$1{,}547$

4.6 Linking Social Media Addiction to Level of Use and Gratifications-Obtained

$H_{2.1}$ proposed that the more the adolescents in urban China use social media, the more likely they will be addicted to social media. As expected, bivariate correlation results in Table 4.7 show the social media addiction index significantly and positively correlated with each kind of social medium use (r ranged from .24 to .40). Furthermore, the four addiction symptoms all significantly and positively associated with each kind of social medium use (r ranged from .05 to .37). Thus, $H_{2.1}$ was strongly supported.

$H_{2.2}$ predicted that the more adolescents in urban China find social media gratifying, the more likely they will be addicted to social media. In Table 4.7, bivariate correlation results show the social media addiction index significantly and positively correlated with all seven gratifications adolescents obtained from social media (r ranged from .06 to .37). Meanwhile, the four addiction symptoms significantly and positively associated with most of the gratification dimensions (r ranged from .06 to .40). Thus, $H_{2.2}$ was supported.

Notably, in Table 4.7, information seeking significantly and negatively correlated with loss of interest in social activities ($r=-.05, p<.05$) and not significantly associated with preoccupation and adverse consequences ($r=.01$, n.s. and $r=-.00$, n.s., respectively). This indicates that information seeking will not likely cause adolescents to be preoccupied with social media and suffer from adverse consequences in their school work or academic performance. In addition, the more engaged in information seeking in social media, the less likely they will lose interest in offline social activities, probably because the information they obtain from social media helps to facilitate their offline sharing and interaction with others. Thus, information seeking can be encouraged. Further, friendship maintenance and peer attention did not significantly correlate with loss of interest in offline social activities ($r=.02$, n.s. and $r=.03$, n.s., respectively). This result suggests that adolescents who maintain friendships and receive peer attention through social media will not lose interest in offline social activities. They not only enjoy friendship and peer attention online but also enjoy them offline as well.

Table 4.7 Summary of the correlation results between social media addiction and level of social media use, gratifications, and parental control

Variable	Social media addiction index	Preoccupation	Adverse consequences	Alleviation of negative emotion	Loss of interest in social activities
Social media use					
IM	.40***	.28***	.29***	.37***	.18***
SNS	.27***	.20***	.19***	.26***	.11***
Blog	.24***	.16***	.14***	.31***	.08**
Microblog	.25***	.18***	.17***	.27***	.05*
Gratifications					
Friendship maintenance	.19***	.12***	.09***	.27***	.02
Social exchange	.20***	.15***	.12***	.25***	.06*
Peer attention	.21***	.15***	.08**	.29***	.03
Free expression	.23***	.15***	.08**	.30***	.10***
Information seeking	.06*	.01	–.00	.12***	–.05*
Identity creation and management	.19***	.17***	.09**	.15***	.17***
Escape	.37***	.27***	.25***	.40***	.18***
Parental control	.15***	.15***	.09***	.07**	.11***

Note: $^{*}p<.05$; $^{**}p<.01$; $^{***}p<.001$. $N=1{,}523$–$1{,}549$

4.7 Linking Social Media Addiction to Parental Control

$H_{2.3}$ proposed that the more strictly parents control adolescent online behavior, the more likely the adolescents will become addicted to social media. Correlation results in Table 4.7 show parental control significantly and positively correlated not only with the adolescent social media addiction index ($r=.15$, $p<.001$) but also with four addiction symptoms (r ranged from .07 to .15). This result reflects the rebellious or contrary nature of adolescents and not surprisingly shows they may not always follow parental guidance. If parents do not allow adolescents free reign to use social media, they may try to find more chances to use it, such as secretly through their mobile phones. Conversely, if adolescents are addicted to social media, their parents will attempt to control their use even more stringently. Thus, $H_{2.3}$ was supported.

This chapter mainly discusses uses, gratifications, and addiction of social media among adolescents in urban China. The next chapter will continue to report survey findings, especially focusing on linking social media addiction to socio-psychological traits.

References

Young, K. S. (1996). *Caught in the net: How to recognize the signs of Internet addiction—and a winning strategy for recovery*. New York: Wiley.

Young, K. S. (1999). Internet addiction: Symptoms, evaluation, and treatment. In L. VandeCreek & T. Jackson (Eds.), *Innovations in clinical practice: A source book* (Vol. 17, pp. 19–31). Sarasota: Professional Resource Press.

Chapter 5
Social Media Addiction and Sociopsychological Traits

This chapter discusses social media addiction from the perspective of sociopsychological traits. It elaborates on the social traits "need for affiliation" and "impression management" and the psychological traits "narcissism" and "leisure boredom" and their relationships with gratifications, level of social media use, and social media addiction. Further, it explores predictors of gratifications, level of social media use, social media addiction, and the corresponding addiction symptoms, as well as discriminating factors of social media addicts and nonaddicts. Implied by the findings, the chapter also examines the mediation effects of gratifications between sociopsychological traits and social media addiction.

5.1 Effects of Need for Affiliation

$H_{3.1}$ hypothesized the stronger the need for affiliation of adolescents in urban China, the more they will find social media gratifying. Bivariate correlation results in Table 5.1 illustrate, as expected, that need for affiliation significantly and positively associated with seven social media gratifications, namely, friendship maintenance ($r=.41, p<.001$), social exchange ($r=.27, p<.001$), peer attention ($r=.35, p<.001$), free expression ($r=.30$, $p<.001$), information seeking ($r=.30$, $p<.001$), identity creation and management ($r=.09, p<.01$), and escape ($r=.22, p<.001$). These indicate that adolescents who have a stronger need for affiliation indeed find social media more gratifying. Thus, $H_{3.1}$ was strongly supported.

$H_{3.2}$ proposed that the stronger the need for affiliation of adolescents in urban China, the more they will use social media. Results in Table 5.1 indicate that need for affiliation indeed had a significant and positive relationship with all four kinds of social medium use including IM ($r=.14$, $p<.001$), SNS ($r=.12$, $p<.001$), blogs ($r=.12$, $p<.001$), and microblogs ($r=.11$, $p<.001$). Thus, adolescents who have a stronger need for affiliation use social media more. Therefore, $H_{3.2}$ was strongly supported.

H. Huang, *Social Media Generation in Urban China: A Study of Social Media Use and Addiction among Adolescents*, Understanding China,
DOI 10.1007/978-3-642-45441-7_5,

Table 5.1 Summary of the correlation results between need for affiliation and gratifications, level of social media use, and social media addiction

	Need for affiliation
Gratifications	
Friendship maintenance	.41***
Social exchange	.27***
Peer attention	.35***
Free expression	.30***
Information seeking	.30***
Identity creation and management	.09**
Escape	.22***
Social media use	
IM	.14***
SNS	.12***
Blogs	.12***
Microblogs	.11***
Social media addiction index	.10***
Addiction symptoms	
Preoccupation	.07*
Adverse consequences	.02
Alleviation of negative emotions	.17***
Loss of interest in social activities	−.06**

Note: *$p<.05$; **$p<.01$; ***$p<.001$. $N=1{,}523$–$1{,}549$

$H_{3.3}$ hypothesized that the stronger the need for affiliation of adolescents, the more likely they will be addicted to social media. Correlation results in Table 5.1 show that the need for affiliation significantly and positively correlated with the social media addiction index ($r=.10, p<.001$). As for addiction symptoms, the need for affiliation positively correlated with preoccupation ($r=.07, p<.05$) and alleviation of negative emotions ($r=.17, p<.001$), negatively correlated with loss of interest in offline social activities ($r=-.06, p<.01$), and did not correlate with adverse consequences ($r=.02$, n.s.). These findings suggest that adolescents who have a strong need for affiliation will not lose interest in offline social activities. They seek affiliation both online through social media and offline through social activities. Meanwhile, need for affiliation does not relate to school performance or productivity impairments caused by excessive social media use. Thus, $H_{3.3}$ was partially supported.

5.2 Impression Management Tactics in Social Media

RQ_5 asked about impression management tactics adolescents use in social media. To answer this research question, principal component factor analysis was run, and it yielded four impression management tactics adolescents used in social media, which accounted for 75.47 % of total variance. As shown in Table 5.2, the first

Table 5.2 Factor analysis of impression management tactics among adolescents

	Mean	SD	Factor 1	2	3	4
Ingratiation						
1. I compliment the experiences of my friends in social media so that they are willing to share with me	3.07	1.05	.85			
2. I praise my friends in social media so that they will see me as friendly	3.08	1.03	.83			
3. I pay attention to my friends in social media so that they would think I care about them	3.21	.98	.82			
Damage control						
4. If I hurt my friend, I will apologize to him/her through social media	3.37	1.16		.91		
5. If I have done something wrong, I will apologize to my friends through social media	3.26	1.14		.89		
6. I offer explanations or justify my behavior for negative events in social media, so as to reduce the negative impression others have of me	3.09	1.13		.74		
Manipulation						
7. When I don't get a good grade, I explain in social media that it's not all my fault	2.10	.98			.84	
8. I depreciate my rival on social media	1.77	.96			.82	
9. When I'm blamed for something, I make excuses on social media	2.69	1.06			.60	
Self-promotion						
10. I share my daily or traveling photos on which I look good with friends in social media	3.00	1.16				.84
11. I share my good scores or positive accomplishments with friends in social media	2.72	1.07				.84
Eigenvalues			4.43	1.55	1.42	.90
Variance explained (%)			22.70	21.42	16.80	14.55
Cronbach's alpha			.87	.85	.70	.75

Note: Scale: 1 = very infrequently and 5 = very frequently. Total variance, 75.47 %. N = 1,535

tactic, "ingratiation" ($\alpha = .87$; eigenvalue = 4.43; explained 22.70 % of the variance), consisted of three items. This tactic reflected adolescents paid attention to their friends, complimented their friends' experiences, and praised their friends in social media to show their friendliness and care. "Damage control," the second tactic ($\alpha = .85$; eigenvalue = 1.55; explained 21.42 % of the variance), included three items characterizing how adolescents reduced negative impressions on social media.

Adolescents apologized to friends if they had done something wrong, or they offered explanations and/or justifications for negative or offensive behavior. "Manipulation," the third tactic ($\alpha = .70$; eigenvalue = 1.42; explained 16.80 % of the variance), consisted of three items illustrating on social media, how adolescents might comment negatively about a rival, make excuses if blamed for something, or rationalize why they received a poor mark. The fourth tactic, "self-promotion" ($\alpha = .75$; eigenvalue = .90; explained 14.55 % of the variance), contained two items indicating that adolescents used social media to share good scores, positive accomplishments, or photos—such as day-to-day or vacation/travel photos—that made them look good. These four tactics revealed the competence of adolescents to present themselves or manage the impression others had of them using social media. Table 5.2 shows the factor loading. The impression management tactics identified from social media agree with traditional impression management skills used in face-to-face communication (Jones and Pittman 1982). They also confirm the self-presentation tactics Jung et al. (2007) found in blogs and Rosenberg (2009) identified in Facebook.

5.3 Effects of Impression Management

$H_{4.1}$ proposed that adolescents who are better at impression management tactics tend to find social media more gratifying. Table 5.3 shows that four impression management tactics significantly and positively correlated with most of the seven gratifications (r ranged from .10 to .40), with the exception of manipulation and information seeking. Table 5.3 shows impression management tactics as strongest when correlating with friendship maintenance, social exchange, and peer attention, the three gratifications categorized as serving social gratifications. This indicates that those adolescents adept at impression management tactics enjoy and are especially satisfied by social gratifications provided by social media. $H_{4.1}$ was supported.

$H_{4.2}$ predicted adolescents who are better at impression management tactics tend to use social media more. Table 5.3 reveals the correlation results illustrating that all four impression management tactics significantly and positively correlated with the level of each kind of social medium use (r ranged from .10 to .28). Thus, $H_{4.2}$ is strongly supported.

$H_{4.3}$ hypothesized that adolescents who are better at impression management tactics are more likely to be addicted to social media. Table 5.3 shows that four impression management tactics positively correlated with the social media addiction index (r ranged from .21 to .36). In terms of social media addiction symptoms, four impression management tactics positively associated with most of the addiction symptoms (r ranged from .07 to .34), except self-promotion and ingratiation were not associated with loss of interest in offline social activities. These results suggest that adolescents who are better at impression management in social media are more likely to be addicted to social media and experience various addiction symptoms. However, those who excel at self-promotion and ingratiation on social media do not necessarily lose interest in offline social activities; they enjoy friendships both

Table 5.3 Summary of the correlation results between impression management and gratifications, level of social media use, and social media addiction

	Self-promotion	Ingratiation	Manipulation	Damage control
Gratifications				
Friendship maintenance	.32***	.40***	.10***	.22***
Social exchange	.30***	.33***	.17***	.24***
Peer attention	.34***	.39***	.15***	.25***
Free expression	.23***	.29***	.11***	.26***
Information seeking	.23***	.27***	−.03	.19***
Identity creation and management	.11***	.12***	.15***	.12***
Escape	.22***	.27***	.21***	.20***
Social media use				
IM	.24***	.22***	.23***	.28***
SNS	.22***	.18***	.11***	.10***
Blogs	.26***	.22***	.14***	.16***
Microblogs	.25***	.20***	.16***	.17***
Social media addiction index	.22***	.21***	.36***	.24***
Addiction symptoms				
Preoccupation	.16***	.14***	.34***	.18***
Adverse consequences	.14***	.10***	.26***	.14***
Alleviation of negative emotions	.27***	.27***	.28***	.24***
Loss of interest in social activities	.04	.03	.22***	.07**

Note: ** $p < .01$; *** $p < .001$. $N = 1{,}532–1{,}549$

online through social media and offline through social activities with friends. As the results shown in Table 5.3 reveal, $H_{4.3}$ was supported.

5.4 Effects of Narcissism

$H_{5.1}$ hypothesized that more narcissistic adolescents tend to find social media more gratifying. Table 5.4 demonstrates three of the four narcissism dimensions, namely, superiority, exploitativeness, and self-absorption, as significantly and positively correlated with most of the seven gratifications (r ranged from .08 to .26). But leadership correlated only with peer attention. These results indicate social media can gratify adolescents who demonstrate superiority, exploitativeness, and self-absorption, but for those who show a strong sense of leadership, social media can only gratify them with peer attention. Thus, $H_{5.1}$ was partially supported.

$H_{5.2}$ hypothesized that more narcissistic adolescents tend to use social media more. Results in Table 5.4 show that superiority, exploitativeness, and self-absorption significantly and positively correlated with each kind of social medium use (r ranged from .08 to .16). However, leadership associated only with SNS and

Table 5.4 Summary of the correlation results between narcissism and gratifications, level of social media use, and social media addiction

	Superiority	Exploitativeness	Self-absorption	Leadership
Gratifications				
Friendship maintenance	.14***	.15***	.20***	−.02
Social exchange	.13***	.17***	.20***	.03
Peer attention	.19***	.25***	.26***	.09**
Free expression	.13***	.10***	.16***	−.01
Information seeking	.17***	.11***	.16***	.00
Identity creation and management	.14***	.03	.13***	−.02
Escape	.09**	.08**	.17***	−.01
Social media use				
IM	.08**	.08**	.11***	.03
SNS	.11***	.11***	.15***	.06*
Blogs	.08**	.08**	.16***	.05
Microblogs	.10***	.09***	.10***	.08**
Social media addiction index	.03	.02	.20***	−.01
Addiction symptoms				
Preoccupation	.04	.04	.15***	.01
Adverse consequences	−.04	−.03	.12***	−.05
Alleviation of negative emotions	.06*	.05*	.23***	.02
Loss of interest in social activities	.00	−.00	.06*	−.04

Note: $*p<.05$; $**p<.01$; $***p<.001$. $N=1{,}529–1{,}549$

microblog use ($r=.06, p<.05$; $r=.08, p<.01$, respectively). Those who had a strong sense of leadership used only more SNS and microblogs. This may be because only SNS and microblogs show the number of friends or followers on one's page, which might satisfy the narcissistic adolescents' sense of leadership. Therefore, $H_{5.2}$ was mostly supported.

$H_{5.3}$ predicted more narcissistic adolescents are more likely to be addicted to social media. Table 5.4 shows only self-absorption as positively correlated with the social media addiction index ($r=.20$, $p<.001$) and all four addiction symptoms (r ranged from .06 to .23). This suggests self-absorbed adolescents eager for others' praise on social media may become addicted to social media. Thus, $H_{5.3}$ was marginally supported.

5.5 Effects of Leisure Boredom

$H_{6.1}$ proposed that adolescents who are more leisurely bored tend to find social media more gratifying. Table 5.5 shows leisure boredom negatively correlated with friendship maintenance ($r=-.06$, $p<.05$), peer attention ($r=-.08$, $p<.01$), and

Table 5.5 Summary of the correlation results between leisure boredom and gratifications, level of social media use, and social media addiction

	Leisure boredom
Gratifications	
Friendship maintenance	−.06*
Social exchange	−.02
Peer attention	−.08**
Free expression	−.03
Information seeking	−.12***
Identity creation and management	.07**
Escape	.07**
Social media use	
IM	.05*
SNS	.01
Blogs	.02
Microblogs	.01
Social media addiction index	.28***
Addiction symptoms	
Preoccupation	.27***
Adverse consequences	.25***
Alleviation of negative emotions	.16***
Loss of interest in social activities	.26***

Note: $^*p<.05$; $^{**}p<.01$; $^{***}p<.001$. N=1,528–1,549

information seeking ($r=-.12$, $p<.001$) but positively correlated with identity creation and management ($r=.07$, $p<.01$) and escape ($r=.07$, $p<.01$). Leisure boredom did not correlate with social exchange ($r=-.02$, n.s.) and free expression ($r=-.03$, n.s.). These results reveal that adolescents who fall prey to leisure boredom receive more gratification from identity creation and management in social media and use social media as an attractive diversion to escape from boredom. Meanwhile, adolescents who maintain friendships, attract peer attention, and seek information on social media are less bored in leisure because they have so many activities in social media. As a result, $H_{6.1}$ is only partially supported.

$H_{6.2}$ suggested that adolescents who are more leisurely bored tend to use social media more. Correlation results revealed that leisure boredom correlated only with IM use ($r=.05$, $p<.05$) but had no relationship with the use of SNS ($r=.01$, n.s.), blogs ($r=.02$, n.s.) or microblogs ($r=.01$, n.s.). This suggests that adolescents who are leisurely bored use IM excessively to pass time, but they do not resort to other social media that much. Thus, $H_{6.2}$ was only partially supported.

$H_{6.3}$ suggested that adolescents who are more leisurely bored are more likely to be addicted to social media. As shown in Table 5.5, results from correlation analyses showed that leisure boredom significantly and positively correlated not only with social media addiction ($r=.28$, $p<.001$) but also with all four addiction symptoms, namely, preoccupation ($r=.27$, $p<.001$), adverse consequences ($r=.25$, $p<.001$), alleviation of negative emotions ($r=.16$, $p<.001$), and loss of interest in offline social activities ($r=.26$, $p<.001$). These results reveal that adolescents who are leisurely bored are more likely to be addicted to social media: they will more likely be preoccupied by social media and will use them excessively to alleviate negative emotions, and they will lose interest in offline social activities and suffer the adverse consequences. Thus, $H_{6.3}$ was strongly supported.

5.6 Predicting Social Media Gratifications

To examine the extent to which demographics and sociopsychological traits (i.e., need for affiliation, impression management, leisure boredom, and narcissism) can predict social media gratifications among adolescents (see RQ_6), seven parallel hierarchical regressions were performed for all types of social media gratifications.

As shown in Table 5.6, demographics such as age and gender were entered into the first block. Being female was significant in predicting friendship maintenance ($\beta = -.09$, $p < .001$), social exchange ($\beta = -.05$, $p < .05$), and peer attention ($\beta = -.10$, $p < .001$), and these three factors were types of gratifications emphasizing the "social" functions of social media. This indicates that girls appreciate the social functions of social media more than boys. This supports Weiser's (2000) finding that females will more likely engage in CMC for social purposes to maintain connections with friends and relatives. Age positively predicted gratifications such as friendship maintenance ($\beta = .11$, $p < .001$), social exchange ($\beta = .07$, $p < .01$), peer attention ($\beta = .10$, $p < .001$), free expression ($\beta = .07$, $p < .01$), and information seeking ($\beta = .11$, $p < .001$) but negatively predicted identity creation and management ($\beta = -.12$, $p < .001$). This suggests that older adolescents tend to obtain more gratifications from social functions such as friendship maintenance, social exchange, and peer attention, as well as from information functions such as information seeking and free expression, while younger adolescents tend to obtain more gratifications from entertainment functions such as identity creation and management. The demographics block explained 0–4 % (as shown in Table 5.6) of the total variance for social media gratifications.

The second block included the psychological variables leisure boredom and narcissism. Leisure boredom was significant in predicting entertainment gratifications of social media, namely, identity creation and management ($\beta = .10$, $p < .001$) and escape ($\beta = .10$, $p < .001$). This indicates that the entertainment functions of social media can satisfy those adolescents who are leisurely bored. They create and manage different identities on social media and consider them places to escape to from boredom and/or bother. Adolescents who had superiority type of personality used social media for information seeking ($\beta = .09$, $p < .01$), as well as for identity creation and management ($\beta = .20$, $p < .001$); exploitative adolescents were more likely to use social media to attract peer attention ($\beta = .10$, $p < .001$) but less likely to use social media for identity creation and management ($\beta = -.12$, $p < .001$); self-absorption was a significant predictor for all seven gratifications, that is, self-absorbed adolescents used social media for friendship maintenance ($\beta = .05$, $p < .05$), social exchange ($\beta = .06$, $p < .05$), peer attention ($\beta = .08$, $p < .01$), free expression ($\beta = .06$, $p < .05$), information seeking ($\beta = .05$, $p < .05$), identity creation and

Table 5.6 Hierarchical regressions of demographics and sociopsychological traits on social media gratifications of adolescents

	Social gratifications						Information gratifications				Entertainment gratifications			
	Friendship maintenance		Social exchange		Peer attention		Free expression		Information seeding		Identity creation and management		Escape	
Predictors	β	ΔR^2	β	ΔR^2	β	ΔR^2	β	ΔR^2	β	ΔR^2	β	ΔR^2	β	ΔR^2
Block 1: Demographics														
Age	.11***		.07**		.10***		.07**		.11***		–.12***		–.00	
Gender (male=1)	–.09***	*.04*	–.05*	*.02*	–.10***	*.04*	–.00	*.01*	–.01	*.02*	–.03	*.01*	–.01	*.00*
Block 2: psychological traits														
Leisure Boredom	.01		.05		–.01		.02		–.05		.10***		.10***	
Narcissism														
Superiority	.02		–.02		–.02		.04		.09**		.20***		–.01	
Expoitativeness	.01		.05		.10***		–.03		–.04		–.12***		–.03	
Self-absorption	.05*		.06*		.08**		.06*		.05*		.10**		.08**	
Leadership	–.09***	*.05*	–.03	*.04*	–.00	*.09*	–.06*	*.03*	–.07**	*.05*	–.08**	*.05*	–.04	*.03*
Block 3: social traits														
Need for affiliation	.30***		.15***		.21***		.21***		.19***		.03		.15***	
Impression management														
Self-promotion	.09***		.12***		.12***		.05		.07*		.02		.06*	
Ingratiation	.23***		.13***		.16***		.14***		.12***		.07*		.12***	
Manipulation	–.03		.05		.01		–.01		–.14***		.07*		.09**	
Damage control	.04	*.20*	.11***	*.12*	.08**	*.14*	.15***	*.12*	.10***	*.10*	.06*	*.02*	.07*	*.10*
R^2		*.29*		*.18*		*.27*		*.16*		*.17*		*.08*		*.13*
Final adjusted R^2		*.28*		*.17*		*.27*		*.16*		*.17*		*.08*		*.13*
F	60.53***		40.86***		62.65***		42.09***		28.47***		15.18***		32.11***	

Note: ***$p<.001$; **$p<.01$; *$p<.05$. $N=1{,}519–1{,}527$

management (β=.10, p<.01), and escape (β=.08, p<.01). However, adolescents who had a strong sense of leadership were less likely to use social media for friendship maintenance (β=−.09, p<.001), free expression (β=−.06, p<.05), information seeking (β=−.07, p<.01), and identity creation and management (β=−.08, p<.01). Thus, different dimensions of narcissism predict different social media gratifications. Generally, this agrees with findings by Bibby (2008) that showed narcissists enjoy the exhibitionistic nature of social media. The psychological traits block accounted for 3–9 % (as indicated in Table 5.6) of the total variance for social media gratifications.

Social traits need for affiliation and impression management were entered in the last block. Need for affiliation was a strong and positive predictor for six types of gratifications, that is, adolescents who had a stronger need for affiliation were more likely to use social media for friendship maintenance (β=.30, p<.001), social exchange (β=.15, p<.001), peer attention (β=.21, p<.001), free expression (β=.21, p<.001), information seeking (β=.19, p<.001), and escape (β=.15, p<.001). This reinforces the previous result that the stronger the need for affiliation of adolescents, the more they find social media gratifying. It also strongly supports Peter and Valkenburg's (2006) affirmation that the greater the adolescents' need for affiliation, the more interpersonal communication gratification they obtain from online communication. Adolescents who excelled at self-promotion used social media mainly for social functions such as friendship maintenance (β=.09, p<.001), social exchange (β=.12, p<.001), peer attention (β=.12, p<.001), information seeking (β=.07, p<.05), and escape (β=.06, p<.05). Those who excelled at ingratiation using social media received all seven types of gratifications: friendship maintenance (β=.23, p<.001), social exchange (β=.13, p<.001), peer attention (β=.16, p<.001), free expression (β=.14, p<.001), information seeking (β=.12, p<.001), identity creation and management (β=.07, p<.05), and escape (β=.12, p<.001). Adolescents adopted manipulation in social media mainly for entertainment functions such as identity creation and management (β=.07, p<.05) and escape (β=.09, p<.01) but not for information seeking (β=−.14, p<.001). Damage control predicted gratifications such as social exchange (β=.11, p<.001), peer attention (β=.08, p<.01), free expression (β=.15, p<.001), information seeking (β=.10, p<.001), identity creation and management (β=.06, p<.05), and escape (β=.07, p<.05). Adolescents who were competent in using different impression management tactics obtained diverse gratifications from social media. This block formed by social traits explained the largest amount of total variance for all seven gratifications except identity creation and management; the variance explained was 20 % for friendship maintenance, 12 % for social exchange, 14 % for peer attention, 12 % for free expression, 10 % for information seeking, 2 % for identity creation and management, and 10 % for escape. Controlling for demographics and psychological traits, social traits constructed the most powerful block to explain most of social media gratifications. This reinforces the social functions of social media for interpersonal communication that satisfy the interpersonal needs of adolescents. These seven regression equations explained 8–28 % (as shown in Table 5.6) of the total variance for seven types of gratifications adolescents obtained from social media.

5.7 Predicting the Level of Social Media Use

To examine the predictability of demographics, parental control, sociopsychological traits of adolescents, and gratifications on the level of use of each social medium (see RQ_7), four paralleled hierarchical regressions were performed.

Results in Table 5.7 show demographics such as age and gender entered into the first block. Boys tended to use more IM and SNS ($\beta=.05$, $p<.05$; $\beta=.05$, $p<.05$), while girls were likely to use more blogs and microblogs ($\beta=-.16$, $p<.001$; $\beta=-.09$, $p<.001$). This suggests certain gender differences in the choice of social media. Compared to boys, girls will more likely write diaries, and thus they may extend this habit to social media, such as writing blogs or microblogs as their online diaries. This agrees with the stereotype of females as more emotionally expressive than males (Brunet and Schmidt 2010). Younger adolescents tended to use IM and blogs more ($\beta=-.05$, $p<.05$; $\beta=-.07$, $p<.01$), while older adolescents tended to use SNS more ($\beta=.08$, $p<.01$). This may be because older adolescents have stronger intentions to build interpersonal networks through SNS. The demographics block explained 0–4 % (as shown in Table 5.7) of the total variance for the level of each social medium use.

The second block included parental control. Surprisingly, parental control had no relationship with the individual kinds of social medium use. This suggests that oftentimes parents fail to effectively control adolescent social media use. This block explained none of the variance.

Psychological traits leisure boredom and narcissism were entered in the third block. Adolescents who were leisurely bored tended to use more IM ($\beta=.06$, $p<.05$) but not the other social media. However, narcissism had no significant effect on adolescents' level of social media use. This block formed by psychological traits accounted for 2 % of the total variance for the level of social media use.

The fourth block includes social traits need for affiliation and impression management. Need for affiliation did not significantly explain the level of social media use. Among four impression management tactics, self-promotion was a significant predictor for the level of each social medium use. That is, adolescents who adept at self-promotion tended to use more IM ($\beta=.11$, $p<.001$), SNS ($\beta=.13$, $p<.001$), blogs ($\beta=.15$, $p<.001$), and microblogs ($\beta=.16$, $p<.001$). Through self-promotion in social media, they could highlight certain aspects of themselves (Marwick 2005) and upload photos conveying the best images of themselves (Ellison et al. 2006). Those who often did manipulation and damage control through social media tended to use more IM ($\beta=.09$, $p<.01$; $\beta=.16$, $p<.001$) and microblogs ($\beta=.10$, $p<.001$; $\beta=.06$, $p<.05$). Compared with SNS and blogs, IM and microblogs are used more for one-to-one communication, thus they may have more effectiveness for manipulation and damage control. This block formed by social traits explained 5–11 % (as indicated in Table 5.7) of the variance for the level of each social medium use.

Social media gratifications were entered last into the equations. Adolescents used SNS and blogs mainly for friendship maintenance ($\beta=.09$, $p<.01$; $\beta=.07$, $p<.05$); they used IM, SNS, and blogs for social exchange ($\beta=.12$, $p<.001$; $\beta=.07$,

Table 5.7 Hierarchical regressions of demographics, parental control, sociopsychological traits, and social media gratifications on level of social media use

	IM		SNS		Blogs		Microblogs	
Predictors	β	ΔR^2	β	ΔR^2	β	ΔR^2	β	ΔR^2
Block 1: demographics								
Age	–.05*		.08**		–.07**		.05	
Gender (male=1)	.05*	*.00*	.05*	*.01*	–.16***	*.04*	–.09***	*.01*
Block 2: parental control	–.03	*.00*	–.01	*.00*	.02	*.00*	.00	*.00*
Block 3:psychological traits								
Leisure boredom	.06*		.03		.04		.02	
Narcissism								
Superiority	.01		.04		–.00		.04	
Exploitativeness	.00		.03		–.02		–.01	
Self-absorption	–.00		.04		.04		–.01	
Leadership	.02	*.02*	.05	*.02*	.02	*.02*	.04	*.02*
Block 4: social traits								
Need for affiliation	.01		.02		–.02		.01	
Impression management								
Self-promotion	.11***		.13***		.15***		.16***	
Ingratiation	–.01		–.01		.04		.01	
Manipulation	.09**		.04		.04		.10***	
Damage control	.16***	*.11*	–.01	*.05*	.05	*.06*	.06*	*.06*
Block 5: gratifications-obtained								
Friendship maintenance	.03		.09**		.07*		.01	
Social exchange	.12***		.07*		.07*		–.02	
Peer attention	.05		.08*		.04		.02	
Free expression	.05		–.11***		.03		.02	
Information seeking	–.03		–.00		.03		.11***	
Identity creation and management	.04		.02		.06*		.02	
Escape	.15***	*.04*	.06*	*.03*	.02	*.02*	.03	*.01*
R^2		*.17*		*.11*		*.14*		*.10*
Final adjusted R^2		*.16*		*.10*		*.13*		*.10*
F	36.85***		15.83***		29.03***		20.71***	

Note: ***$p<.001$; **$p<.01$; *$p<.05$. N=1,495–1,501

$p<.05$; $\beta=.07$, $p<.05$). SNS serve as online public spaces, which provide opportunities for adolescents to attract peer attention ($\beta=.08$, $p<.05$); because adolescents usually used their real names in SNS, lack of anonymity limited free expression in SNS ($\beta=-.11$, $p<.001$). Since the information in microblogs allows for widespread transmitting among followers, adolescents used microblogs mainly for information seeking ($\beta = .11$, $p < .001$). Blogs represent private spaces and owners have full control over their own blogs, so they enjoyed identity creation and management through blogs ($\beta = .06$, $p < .05$). They also considered IM and SNS as good places to use to escape from their problems or worries ($\beta = .15$, $p < .001$; $\beta = .06$, $p < .05$). This block formed by social media gratifications accounted for 1–4 % (as shown in Table 5.7) of the total variance.

To summarize, heavy adolescent users of IM tend to be leisurely bored younger boys who are good at self-promotion, manipulation, and damage control through IM. They receive gratification of social exchange from IM and consider IM a good place to escape from reality. Older boys tend to use SNS more; they are good at self-promotion and enjoy the social functions of SNS, namely, friendship maintenance, social exchange, and peer attention. The limitation of free expression on SNS leaves them dissatisfied because of its lack of anonymity, but they also consider SNS good places to escape from bother and troubles. Heavy users of blogs tend to be younger girls; they are good at self-promotion on blogs, and they use blogs for friendship maintenance, social exchange, and identity creation and management. Girls also tend to use microblogs more; heavy users of microblogs are good at self-promotion, manipulation, and damage control on microblogs, and they use microblogs mainly for information seeking. These four regression equations explained 10–16 % (as indicated in Table 5.7) of the variance for adolescents' level of social media use.

5.8 Profiles of Social Media Addicts

As analyzed above, 15.6 % of the adolescents in this sample could be classified as social media addicts. Compared with nonaddicts, adolescent addicts exhibited significantly heavier daily use of IM, SNS, SNS games, blogs, microblogs, and the Internet; they also had more total friends and more frequent contact friends in IM and SNS and had more followers as well as followings in microblogs. To further distinguish the social media addicts and nonaddicts among adolescents, in terms of demographics, parental control, sociopsychological traits, level of social media use, and gratifications (see RQ_8), discriminant analysis was conducted. Results in Table 5.8 suggest that adolescent social media addicts were distinguished (in the order of strength in the structure coefficients) as using significantly more IM, excelling at impression management tactics, obtaining more escape gratification from social media, experiencing more leisure boredom, and using significantly more SNS, microblogs, and blogs. Therefore, general speaking, adolescent social media addicts are leisurely bored and adept at impression management tactics. They heavily use IM, SNS, blogs, and microblogs and consider social media as ideal places to escape to from their boredom or bother. The function correctly classified 69.4 % of the cases.

Table 5.8 Discriminant analysis of social media addicts with demographics, parental control, sociopsychological traits, social media use, and gratifications as predictors

Predictors	Structure coefficients
Level of use	
IM	.57***
SNS	.39***
Blogs	.30***
Microblogs	.34***
Sociopsychological traits	
Leisure boredom	.49***
Narcissism	.12
Need for affiliation	.25
Impression management	.53***
Gratifications	
Friendship maintenance	.26
Social exchange	.25
Peer attention	.25
Free expression	.27
Information seeking	–.04
Identity creation and management	.29
Escape	.52***
Parental control	.23
Demographics	
Age	–.00
Gender	.05
Eigenvalue	.13
Canonical correlation	.34
Degree of freedom	18
Wilks' lambda	.88
Significance	$p<.001$
Group centroids	
Addicts	.86
Nonaddicts	–.16
Cases correctly classified	69.4 %

Note: ***$p<.001$. $N=1,477$

5.9 Predicting Social Media Addiction and Symptoms

To assess the extent to which demographics, parental control, sociopsychological traits, social media gratifications, and level of social media use can predict social media addiction as well as addiction symptoms (see RQ_9), five parallel hierarchical regressions were performed. As shown in Tables 5.9 and 5.10, demographics were entered first in the first block. Results showed older adolescents more likely to be addict to social media ($\beta=.12$, $p<.001$). They used social media heavily to alleviate negative emotions ($\beta=.08$, $p<.001$) and suffered from adverse consequences ($\beta=.18$, $p<.001$), especially in school performance. Boys were more likely to be preoccupied by social media ($\beta=.07$, $p<.01$), while girls tended to use social media heavily for alleviation of negative emotions ($\beta=-.09$, $p<.001$). The demographics

Table 5.9 Hierarchical regression of demographics, parental control, sociopsychological traits, social media gratifications, and level of social media use on social media addiction

	Model					
	1	2	3	4	5	6
Block 1: demographics						
Age	.10***	.14***	.09***	.11***	.12***	.12***
Gender (male=1)	−.01	−.03	.01	.01	.02	.01
Block 2: parental control		.18***	.15***	.12***	.11***	.12***
Block 3: psychological traits						
Leisure boredom			.27***	.25***	.22***	.21***
Narcissism						
Superiority			.01	−.02	−.02	−.03
Exploitativeness			−.01	−.06	−.05	−.04
Self-absorption			.22***	.14***	.11***	.08***
Leadership			−.02	−.00	.02	−.00
Block 4: social traits						
Need for affiliation				.06*	.02	.00
Impression management						
Self-promotion				.10***	.08**	.02
Ingratiation				.02	−.03	−.03
Manipulation				.25***	.21***	.17***
Damage control				.08**	.06*	.02
Block 5: gratifications-obtained						
Friendship maintenance					.06*	.03
Social exchange					−.02	−.04
Peer attention					.04	.01
Free expression					.06*	.06*
Information seeking					−.11***	−.11***
Identity creation and management					.06*	.04
Escape					.23***	.19***
Block 6: social media use						
IM						.20***
SNS						.12***
Blogs						.05*
Microblogs						.08***
ΔR^2	*.01*	*.03*	*.11*	*.11*	*.07*	*.08*
F	7.64**	21.79***	32.64***	40.43***	36.51***	42.56***
Final adjust R^2						*.40*

Note: *$p<.05$; **$p<.01$; ***$p<.001$. $N=1,488$

Table 5.10 Hierarchical regressions on social media addiction symptoms

	Preoccupation		Adverse consequences		Alleviation of negative emotions		Loss of interest in social activities	
Predictors	β	ΔR^2	β	ΔR^2	β	ΔR^2	β	ΔR^2
Block 1: demographics								
Age	.03		.18***		.08***		.04	
Gender (male = 1)	.07**	*.00*	.02	*.02*	−.09***	*.02*	−.00	*.00*
Block 2: parental control	.10***	*.03*	.09***	*.02*	.05*	*.01*	.06*	*.01*
Block 3: psychological traits								
Leisure boredom	.23***		.18***		.12***		.20***	
Narcissism								
Superiority	−.03		−.08**		−.04		−.00	
Exploitativeness	−.03		−.08**		−.07**		−.00	
Self-absorption	.09***		.04		.09***		.01	
Leadership	−.01	*.10*	−.05*	*.07*	−.02	*.08*	−.02	*.07*
Block 4: social traits								
Need for affiliation	.02		−.01		.03		−.09**	
Impression management								
Self-promotion	−.01		.01		.01		−.04	
Ingratiation	−.03		−.08**		−.01		−.06*	
Manipulation	.18***		.14***		.09***		.12***	
Damage control	.02	*.08*	−.01	*.05*	.04	*.09*	−.04	*.03*
Block 5: gratifications-obtained								
Friendship maintenance	.03		−.02		.03		−.03	
Social exchange	−.02		−.03		−.03		−.04	
Peer attention	.05		−.06*		.03		−.05	
Free expression	.04		−.03		.12***		.08*	
Information seeking	−.10***		−.09***		−.11***		−.11***	
Identity creation and management	.05		.00		−.03		.10***	
Escape	.14***	*.04*	.16***	*.03*	.22***	*.10*	.08**	*.03*
Block 6: social media use								
IM	.11***		.18***		.16***		.08**	
SNS	.10***		.08**		.11***		.06*	
Blogs	.02		.01		.09***		−.01	
Microblogs	.08**	*.03*	.05*	*.04*	.07**	*.07*	−.02	*.01*
R^2		*.28*		*.23*		*.37*		*.15*
Final adjusted R^2		*.27*		*.23*		*.36*		*.15*
F	39.82***		41.00***		47.14***		26.30***	

Note: ***$p<.001$; **$p<.01$; *$p<.05$. N=1,471–1,488

block explained only 1 % of the total variance for adolescent social media addiction and explained no more than 2 % (as shown in Table 5.10) of the total variance for four addiction symptoms.

Parental control was entered next into the equations. Parental control positively predicted not only social media addiction ($\beta = .12$, $p < .001$) but also four addiction symptoms, that is, preoccupation ($\beta = .10$, $p < .001$), adverse consequences ($\beta = .09$, $p < .001$), alleviation of negative emotions ($\beta = .05$, $p < .05$), and loss of interest in offline social activities ($\beta = .06$, $p < .05$). These results suggest that on the one hand, given the somewhat rebellious nature of adolescents, the stricter the parents' control of their social media use, the more they will use them; on the other hand, the more severe the addiction with its attendant various symptoms, the more parents will try to control the adolescent's social media use. Parental control explained 3 % of the total variance for adolescent social media addiction and accounted for 1–3 % (as shown in Table 5.10) of the total variance for the addiction symptoms.

Psychological traits leisure boredom and narcissism went next in the third block. Leisure boredom not only significantly predicted social media addiction ($\beta = .21$, $p < .001$) but also significantly predicted four social media addiction symptoms, namely, preoccupation ($\beta = .23$, $p < .001$), adverse consequences ($\beta = .18$, $p < .001$), alleviation of negative emotions ($\beta = .12$, $p < .001$), and loss of interest in offline social activities ($\beta = .20$, $p < .001$). These data reveal that adolescents who are leisurely bored will indeed more likely be addicted to social media and experience the above four addiction symptoms. As for narcissism, self-absorbed adolescents had a greater likelihood of falling prey to social media addiction ($\beta = .08$, $p < .001$). Narcissism also significantly predicted addiction symptoms. Self-absorbed adolescents were more likely to be preoccupied by social media ($\beta = .09$, $p < .001$) and use social media excessively to alleviate negative emotions ($\beta = .09$, $p < .001$). Those with a sense of superiority, an exploitative nature, and a strong sense of leadership were less likely to suffer from adverse consequences of social media addiction ($\beta = -.08$, $p < .01$; $\beta = -.08$, $p < .01$; $\beta = -.05$, $p < .05$). Further, exploitative adolescents were also less likely to use social media intensively to alleviate negative emotions ($\beta = -.07$, $p < .01$). This block consisting of psychological traits explained 11 % of the total variance for adolescent social media addiction and accounted for 7–10 % (as shown in Table 5.10) of the total variance for addiction symptoms.

In the fourth block, social traits need for affiliation and impression management were entered. Need for affiliation did not significantly predict social media addiction among adolescents, and those who had a strong need for affiliation were not likely to lose interest in offline social activities because of social media addiction ($\beta = -.09$, $p < .01$). For impression management, adolescents who excelled at manipulation through social media had a greater likelihood to be addicted to social media ($\beta = .17$, $p < .001$), to be preoccupied by social media ($\beta = .18$, $p < .001$), and to use them excessively to alleviate negative emotions ($\beta = .09$, $p < .001$), thus suffering from adverse consequences ($\beta = .14$, $p < .001$) and losing interest in offline social activities because of social media addiction ($\beta = .12$, $p < .001$). However, those who did well in ingratiation on social media had a lower likelihood to suffer from adverse consequences ($\beta = -.08$, $p < .01$) and lose interest in offline social activities ($\beta = -.06$, $p < .05$). This block consisting of social traits explained 11 % of the total variance for adolescent social media addiction and accounted for 3–9 % (as shown in Table 5.10) of the total variance for the addiction symptoms.

Seven gratifications-obtained from social media were entered next in the fifth block. Information seeking was not likely to lead to social media addiction ($\beta = -.11$, $p < .001$), instead, free expression and escape were very likely to lead to addiction ($\beta = .06$, $p < .05$; $\beta = .19$, $p < .001$). Social media gratifications also significantly predicted some addiction symptoms. Adolescents who enjoyed free expression in social media used them heavily to alleviate negative emotions ($\beta = .12$, $p < .001$), resulting in losing interest in offline social activities ($\beta = .08$, $p < .05$). Those who enjoyed identity creation and management in social media tended to lose interest in offline social activities ($\beta = .10$, $p < .001$). Furthermore, adolescents who used social media mainly for escaping from problems and worries were very likely to suffer from all kinds of addiction symptoms. They tended to be preoccupied by social media ($\beta = .14$, $p < .001$) and used social media intensively to alleviate negative emotions ($\beta = .22$, $p < .001$), thus these adolescents would suffer from adverse consequences ($\beta = .16$, $p < .001$) and lose interest in offline social activities ($\beta = .08$, $p < .01$). On the contrary, adolescents who acquired peer attention in social media would less likely suffer from adverse consequences ($\beta = -.06$, $p < .05$). Those who enjoyed information seeking in social media were not likely to experience any addiction symptoms. Since they were not preoccupied by social media ($\beta = -.10$, $p < .001$) and did not use social media excessively to alleviate negative emotions ($\beta = -.11$, $p < .001$), as a result, they would not suffer from adverse consequences ($\beta = -.09$, $p < .001$) and lose interest in offline social activities ($\beta = -.11$, $p < .001$). This block consisting of social media gratifications explained 7 % of the total variance for adolescent social media addiction and accounts for 3–10 % (as shown in Table 5.10) of the total variance for the addiction symptoms.

The levels of social media use were entered last in the sixth block. Heavy use of each kind of social media, such as IM ($\beta = .20$, $p < .001$), SNS ($\beta = .12$, $p < .001$), blogs ($\beta = .05$, $p < .05$), and microblogs ($\beta = .08$, $p < .001$), positively predicted social media addiction. Heavy users of IM, SNS, and microblogs were more likely to be preoccupied by them ($\beta = .11$, $p < .001$; $\beta = .10$, $p < .001$; and $\beta = .08$, $p < .01$, respectively) and suffered from adverse consequences ($\beta = .18$, $p < .001$; $\beta = .08$, $p < .01$; and $\beta = .05$, $p < .05$, respectively). Addicts used all four kinds of social media excessively to alleviate negative emotions ($\beta = .16$, $p < .001$; $\beta = .11$, $p < .001$; $\beta = .09$, $p < .001$; and $\beta = .07$, $p < .01$, respectively), while the heavy users of IM ($\beta = .08$, $p < .01$) and SNS ($\beta = .06$, $p < .05$) showed a greater likelihood to lose interest in offline social activities. This block consisting of the level of social media use explained 8 % of the total variance for adolescent social media addiction and accounted for 1–7 % (as shown in Table 5.10) of the total variance for the addiction symptoms.

Generally speaking, adolescents who experience severe social media addiction are older adolescents who are very bored in leisure. Although their parents control their social media use strictly, they still heavily use IM, SNS, blogs, and microblogs. They are self-absorbed and excel at manipulation through social media. They are less likely to use social media for information seeking, but they enjoy free expression in social media and consider social media good places in which to escape their boredom and bother.

Adolescents more likely to be preoccupied by social media tend to be leisurely bored, self-absorbed boys. Despite their parents' severe control of their social media use, they still use IM, SNS, and microblogs heavily. Good at manipulation through social media, they use social media mainly for escape. They will less likely use social media for information seeking.

Students who suffer from adverse consequences such as poor school performance because of social media addiction tend to be less narcissistic but very bored-in-leisure older adolescents. Although parents severely control their social media use, they still use IM, SNS, and microblogs heavily for escaping from boredom and bother. Good at manipulation in social media, they do not do well at ingratiation. They will less likely use social media for information seeking and peer attention.

Those adolescents addicted to social media for alleviation of negative emotions tend to be older girls. Leisurely bored, they are also self-absorbed but not exploitative. Parents also control their social media, but the adolescents still heavily use all kinds of social media. They do well at manipulation in social media. They enjoy free expression through social media and use them for escape but not for information seeking.

Adolescents who lose interest in offline social activities because of social media addiction tend to be those who have less need for affiliation and who are very bored in their leisure time. They use IM and SNS heavily and ignore parental control. Good at manipulation through social media, they do not do well at ingratiation. They use social media for free expression and escape. They are less likely to use social media for information seeking. They do have an interest in identity creation and impression management through social media but not in offline social activities.

These regression equations explained 40 % of the variance for adolescent social media addiction, while accounting for 15–36 % (as indicated in Table 5.10) of the variance for four addiction symptoms. Among them, sociopsychological traits explain the largest amount of variance.

5.10 Mediating Role of Social Media Gratifications

In discriminant analysis, the social trait need for affiliation and the psychological trait narcissism did not significantly distinguish between social media addicts and nonaddicts. However, previous bivariate correlation tests showed the need for affiliation and self-absorption in narcissism significantly correlated with both social media gratifications and social media addiction. Further, it is remarkable to note from the hierarchical regression shown in Table 5.9 that, when social media gratifications were entered into the equation, the effects of sociopsychological traits on social media addiction diminished, especially the effects from the need for affiliation and self-absorption in narcissism. Therefore, this implies certain mediation effects of gratifications acting between sociopsychological traits and social media addiction and merits further investigation.

According to Baron and Kenny (1986), the criteria to establish mediation effects include the following. First, the independent variable (IV) must affect the mediator (M); second, the IV must affect dependent variable (DV); and third, the M must affect the DV, even after the IV is included, and the effect of IV on DV must be less in the third step than in the second. Therefore, a series of regression tests were conducted to examine the possible mediation effects.

As mentioned in the previous chapter, among seven social media gratifications, friendship maintenance, social exchange, and peer attention can be categorized as fulfilling social gratifications; free expression and information seeking can be considered information gratifications; while identity creation and management and escape can be seen as serving entertainment gratifications. To make the gratifications more integrated and manageable and at the same time differentiate the effects of different gratifications, in mediation tests, composite three dimensions of social media gratifications were used as mediators instead of the individual seven types.

5.10.1 *Gratifications as Mediators Between Need for Affiliation and Social Media Addiction*

Inspired by the previous findings, this study further examined the mediation effects of gratifications on need for affiliation and social media addiction. To examine whether social gratifications acted as a mediator between need for affiliation and social media addiction, a series of regressions were performed. Results in Table 5.11 show that need for affiliation (IV) significantly explained social gratifications (M) (β=.42, p<.001) and social media addiction (DV) (β=.10, p<.001) and social gratifications (M) significantly affected social media addiction (DV) (β=.25, p<.001). Controlling for social gratifications, the effect of need for affiliation on addiction decreased to none (β=.00, n.s.), but social gratifications continued to significantly predict social media addiction (β=.25, p<.001). The Sobel test indicated the mediation effect was significant (z=8.10, p<.001). If by adding the mediator, the previous effect IV on DV decreases to zero, it can be considered as full mediation (Baron and Kenny 1986). Therefore, social gratifications acted as a full mediator between need for affiliation and social media addiction.

Similarly, tests were performed to examine whether information gratifications mediated need for affiliation and social media addiction. Table 5.12 shows that need for affiliation (IV) significantly explained information gratifications (M) (β=.35, p<.001) and social media addiction (DV) (β=.10, p<.001); information gratifications (M) significantly affected social media addiction (DV) (β=.17, p<.001). Controlling for information gratifications, the effect of need for affiliation on addiction decreased to insignificance (β=.05, n.s.), but information gratifications continued to significantly predict social media addiction (β=.15, p<.001). The Sobel test indicated a significant mediation effect (z=6.07, p<.001). This

Table 5.11 Regression equations testing the mediation effects of social gratifications between need for affiliation and social media addiction

Eq	Step	Variable entered	*B*	SE	*β*	*t*	ΔR^2	Total R^2
Regressing the mediator on the IV								
a.	1	Need for affiliation	.84	.05	.42	17.89***	.17	.17
Regressing the DV on the mediator								
b.	1	Social gratifications	.37	.04	.25	9.84***	.06	.06
Regressing the DV on the IV								
c.	1	Need for affiliation	.31	.08	.10	3.89***	.01	.01
Regressing the DV on both the IV and the mediator								
d1	1	Need for affiliation	.31	.08	.10	3.89***	.01	.01
	2	Need for affiliation	.00	.09	.00	.05	.05	.06
		Social gratifications	.38	.04	.25	8.95***		
d2	1	Social gratifications	.37	.04	.25	9.84***	.06	.06
	2	Social gratifications	.37	.04	.25	8.95***	.00	.06
		Need for affiliation	.00	.09	.00	.05		

Note: ***$p<.001$. $N=1{,}515$

Table 5.12 Regression equations testing the mediation effects of information gratifications between need for affiliation and social media addiction

Eq	Step	Variable entered	*B*	SE	*β*	*t*	ΔR^2	Total R^2
Regressing the mediator on the IV								
a.	1	Need for affiliation	.39	.03	.35	14.90***	.13	.13
Regressing the DV on the mediator								
b.	1	Information gratifications	.48	.07	.17	6.65***	.03	.03
Regressing the DV on the IV								
c.	1	Need for affiliation	.31	.08	.10	3.89***	.01	.01
Regressing the DV on both the IV and the mediator								
d1	1	Need for affiliation	.31	.08	.10	3.89***	.01	.01
	2	Need for affiliation	.14	.08	.05	1.69	.02	.03
		Information gratifications	.43	.08	.15	5.65***		
d2	1	Information gratifications	.48	.07	.17	6.65***	.03	.03
	2	Information gratifications	.43	.08	.15	5.65***	.00	.03
		Need for affiliation	.14	.08	.05	1.69		

Note: ***$p<.001$. $N=1{,}525$

suggested that information gratifications mediated the relationship between need for affiliation and social media addiction.

Another tests examined whether entertainment gratifications acted as a mediator between need for affiliation and social media addiction. Table 5.13 demonstrates that need for affiliation (IV) significantly predicted entertainment gratifications (M) ($\beta=.18$, $p<.001$) and social media addiction (DV) ($\beta=.10$, $p<.001$) and entertainment gratifications (M) significantly affected social media addiction (DV) ($\beta=.34$, $p<.001$). When entertainment gratifications was controlled, the effect of need for

Table 5.13 Regression equations testing the mediation effects of entertainment gratifications between need for affiliation and social media addiction

Eq	Step	Variable entered	*B*	SE	*β*	*t*	ΔR^2	Total R^2
Regressing the mediator on the IV								
a.	1	Need for affiliation	.23	.03	.18	7.24***	.03	.03
Regressing the DV on the mediator								
b.	1	Entertainment gratifications	.84	.06	.34	13.94***	.11	.11
Regressing the DV on the IV								
c.	1	Need for affiliation	.31	.08	.10	3.89***	.01	.01
Regressing the DV on both the IV and the mediator								
d1	1	Need for affiliation	.31	.08	.10	3.89***	.01	.01
	2	Need for affiliation	.14	.08	.04	1.80	.11	.12
		Entertainment gratifications	.82	.06	.33	13.42***		
d2	1	Entertainment gratifications	.84	.06	.34	13.94***	.11	.11
	2	Entertainment gratifications	.82	.06	.33	13.42***	.01	.12
		Need for affiliation	.14	.08	.04	1.80		

Note: ***$p<.001$. $N=1{,}520$

affiliation on addiction decreased to insignificant ($\beta=.04$, n.s.), but entertainment gratifications remained significant in predicting social media addiction ($\beta=.33$, $p<.001$). The Sobel test indicated a significant mediation effect ($z=6.72$, $p<.001$). As a result, entertainment gratifications mediated need for affiliation and social media addiction.

To summarize, results from the above analyses revealed that all three dimensions of social media gratifications, namely, social, information, and entertainment, all served as significant mediators between need for affiliation and social media addiction, with social gratifications having the strongest mediating effect. This indicates that need for affiliation might not necessarily lead to social media addiction, but those adolescents with a strong need for affiliation, who at the same time obtained plenty of social, information, and entertainment gratifications from social media use, will likely be addicted. Figure 5.1 shows the mediation effects of gratifications on need for affiliation and social media addiction.

5.10.2 *Gratifications as Mediators Between Narcissism and Social Media Addiction*

A series of regression tests were also performed to examine whether gratifications served as mediators between narcissism and social media addiction. Table 5.14 shows how social gratifications mediated narcissism and social media addiction. Results showed that narcissism (IV) significantly explained social gratifications (M) ($\beta=.25$, $p<.001$) and social media addiction (DV) ($\beta=.08$, $p<.01$) and social gratifications (M) significantly affected social media addiction (DV) ($\beta=.25$, $p<.001$).

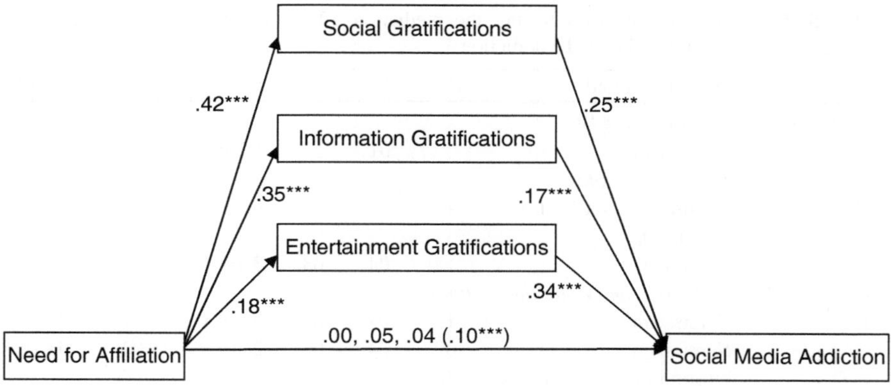

Fig. 5.1 Mediation effects of gratifications between need for affiliation and social media addiction

Table 5.14 Regression equations testing the mediation effects of social gratifications between narcissism and social media addiction

Eq	Step	Variable entered	*B*	SE	*β*	*t*	ΔR^2	Total R^2
Regressing the mediator on the IV								
a.	1	Narcissism	.26	.03	.25	10.19***	.06	.06
Regressing the DV on the mediator								
b.	1	Social gratifications	.37	.04	.25	9.84***	.06	.06
Regressing the DV on the IV								
c.	1	Narcissism	.13	.04	.08	3.26**	.01	.01
Regressing the DV on both the IV and the mediator								
d1	1	Narcissism	.13	.04	.08	3.26**	.01	.01
	2	Narcissism	.04	.04	.02	.90	.05	.06
		Social gratifications	.37	.04	.24	9.33***		
d2	1	Social gratifications	.37	.04	.25	9.84***	.06	.06
	2	Social gratifications	.37	.04	.24	9.33***	.00	.06
		Narcissism	.04	.04	.02	.90		

Note: $^{**}p<.01$; $^{***}p<.001$. $N=1{,}508$

Controlling for social gratifications, the effect of narcissism on addiction diminished to insignificant ($\beta=.02$, n.s.), but social gratifications continued to significantly predict social media addiction ($\beta=.24$, $p<.001$). The Sobel test suggested a significant mediation effect ($z=6.32$, $p<.001$). Thus, social gratifications serve as a mediator between narcissism and social media addiction.

As for information gratifications, Table 5.15 reveals that narcissism (IV) significantly explained information gratifications (M) ($\beta=.17$, $p<.001$) and social media addiction (DV) ($\beta=.08$, $p<.01$) and information gratifications (M) significantly affected social media addiction (DV) ($\beta=.17$, $p<.001$). Controlling for information

Table 5.15 Regression equations testing the mediation effects of information gratifications between narcissism and social media addiction

Eq	Step	Variable entered	*B*	SE	*β*	*t*	ΔR^2	Total R^2
Regressing the mediator on the IV								
a.	1	Narcissism	.09	.01	.17	6.75***	.03	.03
Regressing the DV on the mediator								
b.	1	Information gratifications	.48	.07	.17	6.65***	.03	.03
Regressing the DV on the IV								
c.	1	Narcissism	.13	.04	.08	3.26**	.01	.01
Regressing the DV on both the IV and the mediator								
d1	1	Narcissism	.13	.04	.08	3.26**	.01	.01
	2	Narcissism	.09	.04	.06	2.17*	.02	.03
		Information gratifications	.46	.07	.16	6.29***		
d2	1	Information gratifications	.48	.07	.17	6.65***	.03	.03
	2	Information gratifications	.46	.07	.16	6.29***	.00	.03
		Narcissism	.09	.04	.06	2.17*		

Note: $*p<.05$; $**p<.01$; $***p<.001$. $N=1,517$

Table 5.16 Regression equations testing the mediation effects of entertainment gratifications between narcissism and social media addiction

Eq	Step	Variable entered	*B*	SE	*β*	*t*	ΔR^2	Total R^2
Regressing the mediator on the IV								
a.	1	Narcissism	.08	.02	.14	5.31***	.02	.02
Regressing the DV on the mediator								
b.	1	Entertainment gratifications	.84	.06	.34	13.94***	.11	.11
Regressing the DV on the IV								
c.	1	Narcissism	.13	.04	.08	3.26**	.01	.01
Regressing the DV on both the IV and the mediator								
d1	1	Narcissism	.13	.04	.08	3.26**	.01	.01
	2	Narcissism	.06	.04	.04	1.66	.11	.12
		Entertainment gratifications	.83	.06	.33	13.63***		
d2	1	Entertainment gratifications	.84	.06	.34	13.94***	.11	.11
	2	Entertainment gratifications	.83	.06	.33	13.63***	.01	.12
		Narcissism	.06	.04	.04	1.66		

Note: $**p<.01$; $***p<.001$. $N=1,512$

gratifications, the effect of narcissism on addiction decreased ($\beta=.06$, $p<.05$), and information gratifications still significantly predicted social media addiction ($\beta=.16$, $p<.001$). The Sobel test indicated a significant mediation effect ($z=5.45$, $p<.001$). Therefore, information gratifications performed partial mediation between narcissism and social media addiction.

Entertainment gratifications as a mediator was examined next. Results in Table 5.16 show that narcissism (IV) significantly predicted entertainment

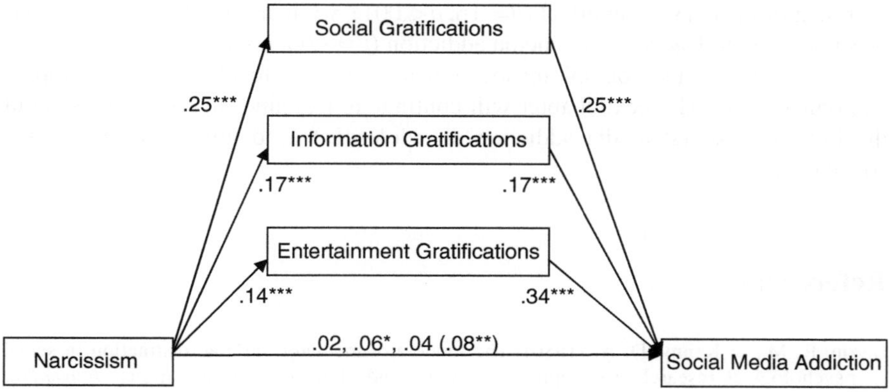

Fig. 5.2 Mediation effects of gratifications between narcissism and social media addiction

gratifications (M) ($\beta = .14$, $p < .001$) and social media addiction (DV) ($\beta = .08$, $p < .01$) and entertainment gratifications (M) significantly affected social media addiction (DV) ($\beta = .34$, $p < .001$). When entertainment gratifications was controlled, the effect of narcissism on addiction decreased to insignificance ($\beta = .04$, n.s.), but entertainment gratifications remained significant to predict social media addiction ($\beta = .33$, $p < .001$). The Sobel test indicated a significant mediation effect ($z = 3.85$, $p < .001$). Hence, entertainment gratifications serve as a mediator between narcissism and social media addiction.

To summarize, the above analyses revealed that all three gratification dimensions mediated the relationship between narcissism and social media addiction, with social gratifications having the strongest mediating effect. This suggests that narcissistic adolescents are not necessarily addicted to social media; only if they are largely gratified by social media in social, information, and entertainment aspects, they will likely be addicted. Figure 5.2 shows the mediation effects of gratifications on narcissism and social media addiction.

The above analyses reveal the mediating role of three dimensions of social media gratifications between need for affiliation, narcissism, and social media addiction. In fact, gratifications also mediated leisure boredom and addiction, as well as impression management and addiction. Given the strong direct effects of leisure boredom and impression management on social media addiction, the mediation effects are relatively weak and therefore not discussed here. But still, the mediation tests above indicate that gratifications mediate between sociopsychological traits and social media addiction. This suggests that if largely satisfied by social media in social, information, and entertainment aspects, adolescents with certain sociopsychological traits are likely to be addicted to social media.

Moreover, it is worthy to note that if three dimensions of gratifications were entered simultaneous into the equation for predicting social media addiction, entertainment gratifications had the most power ($\beta = .30$, $p < .001$); social media gratifications had a weaker effect ($\beta = .16, p < .001$); while information gratifications was not likely to lead to social media addiction ($\beta = -.06$, n.s.).

This chapter focuses on linking social media addiction to adolescents' sociopsychological traits. The next chapter will continue to examine survey findings about the impact of social media addiction on adolescent academic performance and social capital.

References

Baron, R. M., & Kenny, D. A. (1986). The moderator-mediator variable distinction in social psychological research: Conceptual, strategic, and statistical considerations. *Journal of Personality and Social Psychology, 51*(6), 1173–1182.

Bibby, P. A. (2008). Dispositional factors in the use of social networking sites: Findings and implications for social computing research. *Lecture Notes in Computer Science, 5075*, 392–400.

Brunet, P. M., & Schmidt, L. A. (2010). Sex differences in the expression and use of computer-mediated affective language. *Social Science Computer Review, 28*(2), 194–205.

Ellison, N., Heino, R., & Gibbs, J. (2006). Managing impressions online: Self-presentation processes in the online dating environment. *Journal of Computer-Mediated Communication, 11*, 415–441.

Jones, E. E., & Pittman, T. S. (1982). Toward a general theory of strategic self-presentation. In J. Suls (Ed.), *Psychological perspectives on the self* (Vol. 1, pp. 231–262). Hillsdale: Lawrence Erlbaum.

Jung, T., Youn, H., & McClung, S. (2007). Motivations and self-presentation strategies on Korean-based "Cyworld" weblog format personal homepages. *CyberPsychology and Behavior, 10*(1), 24–31.

Marwick, A. (2005, October). *I'm a lot more interesting than a Friendster profile: Identity, authenticity, and power in social networking services.* Paper presented at the conference of Association for Internet Researchers 6, Chicago, IL, USA.

Peter, J., & Valkenburg, P. M. (2006). Research note: Individual differences in perceptions of Internet communication. *European Journal of Communication, 21*(2), 213–226.

Rosenberg, J. (2009). *Online impression management: Personality traits and concern for secondary goals as predictors of self-presentation tactics on Facebook.* Unpublished master's thesis. Kent State University, Kent, OH, USA.

Weiser, E. (2000). Gender differences in Internet use patterns and Internet application preferences: A two-sample comparison. *CyberPsychology & Behavior, 3*(2), 167–178.

Chapter 6
Social Media Addiction, Academic Performance, and Social Capital

Chapters 4 and 5 discussed social media addiction among adolescents in urban China from both the U&G perspective and the effects of sociopsychological traits. Given the widespread and ever-increasing use of social media among adolescents, parents, educators, and society in general must pay more attention to the impact of social media addiction on adolescents. Do adolescents benefit from various kinds of social media? Do they suffer any negative consequences because of social media addiction? This chapter examines the impact of social media on adolescent academic performance and social capital.

6.1 Linking Social Media Addiction to Academic Performance

Academic learning is the major task of adolescents. Academic performance is very important for adolescents because it represents nearly the sole standard deciding what kind of university adolescents can or will eventually enter or how they will eventually make their livelihoods. For this reason, parents and teachers pay much attention to adolescent academic performance. $H_{7.1}$ predicted that the more adolescents use social media, the more likely their academic performance will be negatively affected, while $H_{7.2}$ suggested that the more severely the adolescents are addicted to social media, the more likely their academic performance will suffer. Correlation results in Table 6.1 show that only heavy IM use related negatively to adolescent academic performance ($r=-.20$, $p<.001$). Further, it shows no relationship between academic performance and adolescent use of SNS, blogs, or microblogs. However, adolescent academic performance not only negatively linked to social media addiction ($r=-.16$, $p<.001$) but also to four addiction symptoms, namely, preoccupation ($r=-.12$, $p<.001$), adverse consequences ($r=-.22$, $p<.001$), alleviation of negative emotions ($r=-.05$, $p<.05$), and loss of interest in offline social activities ($r=-.09$, $p<.001$). These results suggest that, although only heavy

H. Huang, *Social Media Generation in Urban China: A Study of Social Media Use and Addiction among Adolescents*, Understanding China,
DOI 10.1007/978-3-642-45441-7_6, © Springer-Verlag Berlin Heidelberg 2014

Table 6.1 Summary of the correlation results between academic performance and social media use and social media addiction

	Academic performance
Social media use	
IM	–.20***
SNS	.01
Blogs	.04
Microblogs	–.03
Social media addiction index	–.16***
Social media addiction symptoms	
Preoccupation	–.12***
Adverse consequences	–.22***
Alleviation of negative emotions	–.05*
Loss of interest in social activities	–.09***

Note: $^{*}p < .05$; $^{***}p < .001$. $N = 1{,}523–1{,}547$

IM use has a negative relationship with adolescent academic performance, if adolescents indulge in social media, become addicted, and show various addiction symptoms, their academic performance will suffer. Thus, $H_{7.1}$ was partially supported, and $H_{7.2}$ was fully supported.

6.2 Predicting Adolescent Academic Performance: A Gender Comparison

To assess controlling for demographics, parental control, and sociopsychological traits, the extent to which gratifications, the level of social media use, and social media addiction can predict adolescent academic performance (see RQ_{10}), hierarchical regression was performed. To further explore any gender differences, boys and girls were separated in different regressions.

Table 6.2 shows demographics entered first into the equation. Results showed that younger adolescents, both among boys and girls, performed better in school ($\beta = -.15$, $p < .001$, and $\beta = -.19$, $p < .001$, respectively). This probably happens because compared with lower grades, the knowledge and exams in upper grades become more complex and difficult so as to distinguish different levels of students. The demographics block explained 2 % and 3 % of the variance for boys and girls, respectively. Parental control was entered next in the second block. Parental control did not have any effect on adolescent academic performance ($\beta = -.03$, n.s., and $\beta = -.06$, n.s., respectively), and this block did not account for any variance explained for boys, while it explained only 1 % of the variance for girls.

Sociopsychological traits were entered next into the equation. Results showed that adolescents, whether boys or girls, who experienced leisure boredom did not perform well in school ($\beta = -.14$, $p < .001$, and $\beta = -.09$, $p < .05$, respectively). This supports the finding of Wegner and colleagues (2008) that high school students who

Table 6.2 Hierarchical regressions of demographics, parental control, sociopsychological traits, gratifications, level of social media use, and social media addiction on adolescent academic performance

	Academic performance—boys		Academic performance—girls	
Predictors	β	ΔR^2	β	ΔR^2
Block 1: demographics				
Age	–.15***	*.02*	–.19***	*.03*
Block 2: parental control	–.03	*.00*	–.06	*.01*
Block 3: sociopsychological traits				
Leisure boredom	–.14***		–.09*	
Narcissism	.08*		.13***	
Need for affiliation	.06		.05	
Impression management	–.02	*.05*	.07	*.04*
Block 4: gratifications-obtained				
Friendship maintenance	.10*		.04	
Social exchange	–.04		–.01	
Peer attention	.03		.02	
Free expression	–.04		.00	
Information seeking	.06		.10**	
Identity creation and management	.02		.03	
Escape	–.12**	*.03*	–.03	*.01*
Block 5: social media use				
IM	–.22***		–.17***	
SNS	.10**		.01	
Blog	.06		.02	
Microblog	–.00	*.05*	.00	*.04*
Block 6: social media addiction				
Preoccupation	.01		.02	
Adverse consequences	–.18***		–.12**	
Alleviation of negative emotions	.15**		.04	
Loss of interest in social activities	.04	*.02*	.01	*.01*
R^2		*.17*		*.14*
Final adjusted R^2		*.16*		*.13*
F	15.49***		14.26***	

Note: ***$p<.001$; **$p<.01$; *$p<.05$. $N=756$ and 702

experienced leisure boredom were not active in learning activities, thus did not perform well in school, and even dropped out of school. However, narcissistic boys and girls tended to have relatively good academic performance ($\beta=.08$, $p<.05$, and $\beta=.13$, $p<.001$, respectively). This falls in line with the previous finding that narcissism, especially superiority, associated with better school grades among adolescents (Aalsma et al. 1997). This block accounted for 5 % and 4 % of the total variance for boys and girls, respectively.

Social media gratifications were entered in the fourth block. Results revealed that if boys used social media for friendship maintenance ($\beta=.10$, $p<.05$), their academic performance would benefit from social media use—probably because friendship maintenance through social media may further facilitate cooperative learning or group discussion among boys. But if boys used social media to escape from problems or difficulties in their studies, social media could negatively affect their academic performance ($\beta = -.12$, $p < .01$). However, information seeking in social media helped girls improve studies ($\beta = .10$, $p < .01$). This block accounted for 3 % and 1 % of the total variance for boys and girls, respectively.

The level of each kind of social medium use was entered next in the fifth block. Results showed that although SNS use could somehow increase boys' academic performance ($\beta = .10$, $p < .01$), heavy use of IM had a negative impact on academic work of both boys and girls ($\beta = -.22$, $p < .001$, and $\beta = -.17$, $p < .001$, respectively). This block also explained 5 % and 4 % of the total variance for boys and girls, respectively.

Social media addiction symptoms were entered last into the equations. Results demonstrated that adolescent social media addicts, both boys and girls, who self-reported that they suffered from adverse consequences due to excessive social media use, indeed performed worse academically ($\beta = -.18$, $p < .001$, and $\beta = -.12$, $p < .01$, respectively) as compared to nonaddicts. However, although previous tests showed that alleviation of negative emotions reversely correlated with adolescents' academic performance, it was interesting to note from regression that if boys often used social media to alleviate negative emotions, it may do good to their academic performance ($\beta = .15$, $p < .01$). This may suggest a gender difference that, if boys use social media intensively for relieving dysphoric moods or escaping from disturbing thoughts, it may help to relieve their study pressure and refresh them, and further facilitates their study. This block accounted for 2 % and 1 % of the total variance for boys and girls, respectively. Overall, the regression equations explained 16 % and 13 % of the variance for boys and girls, respectively.

To summarize, controlling for demographics, parental control, and sociopsychological traits, social media addiction and the excessive use of IM indeed have negative impact on adolescent academic performance. However, boys who use SNS mainly for friendship maintenance but not for escape and girls who use social media mainly for information seeking perform better in school.

6.3 Linking Social Media Addiction to Social Capital

$H_{8.1}$ proposed that the more adolescents use social media, the more social capital they will have. Correlation results in Table 6.3 indicate both bonding and bridging social capital significantly and positively correlated with each kind of social medium use, although not strongly. The more use of IM ($r = .09$, $p < .01$), SNS ($r = .09$, $p < .001$), blogs ($r = .12$, $p < .001$), and microblogs ($r = .08$, $p < .01$), the more bonding social capital adolescents have. Similarly, the more use of IM ($r = .10$, $p < .001$), SNS ($r = .12$, $p < .001$), blogs ($r = .13$, $p < .001$), and microblogs ($r = .12$, $p < .001$), the more bridging capital adolescents report. Thus, $H_{8.1}$ was fully supported.

Table 6.3 Summary of the correlation results between social capital and social media use, social media addiction

	Bonding social capital	Bridging social capital
Social media use		
IM	.09**	.10***
SNS	.09***	.12***
Blogs	.12***	.13***
Microblogs	.08**	.12***
Social media addiction index	–.01	.04
Social media addiction symptoms		
Preoccupation	–.08**	–.00
Adverse consequences	–.04	–.01
Alleviation of negative emotions	.10***	.15***
Loss of interest in social activities	–.17***	–.14***

Note: $^{**}p<.01$; $^{***}p<.001$. $N=1{,}522–1{,}547$

$H_{8.2}$ suggested that the more severely the adolescents are addicted to social media, the more likely their social capital will decrease. However, as shown in Table 6.3, bivariate correlations suggested that both bonding and bridging social capital did not correlate with the social media addiction index, but they did associate with some of the social media addiction symptoms. For example, preoccupation negatively associated with bonding social capital ($r=-.08$, $p<.01$), alleviation of negative emotions had a positive correlation with both bonding ($r=.10$, $p<.001$) and bridging social capital ($r=.15$, $p<.001$), while loss of interest in offline social activities had a negative association with both bonding ($r=-.17$, $p<.001$) and bridging social capital ($r=-.14$, $p<.001$). These results reveal that the level of social media addiction may not have settled positive or negative impact on adolescent social capital. If adolescents are preoccupied by social media, their bonding social capital will be decreased, and if they lose interest in offline social activities because of social media addiction, both their bonding and bridging social capital will decrease as well. But if they turn to heavy use of social media for alleviation of negative emotions, their bonding and bridging social capital will possibly increase. As a result, $H_{8.2}$ was not supported.

6.4 Predicting Social Capital of Adolescents: A Gender Comparison

To examine controlling for demographics and sociopsychological traits, the extent to which gratifications, the level of social media use, and social media addiction can predict both the bonding and bridging social capital of adolescents (see RQ_{11}), as well as to explore any gender differences, four paralleled hierarchical regressions were performed.

Table 6.4 Hierarchical regressions of demographics, sociopsychological traits, gratifications, level of use, and social media addiction on adolescent bonding social capital

	Bonding social capital—boys		Bonding social capital—girls	
Predictors	β	ΔR^2	β	ΔR^2
Block 1: demographics				
Age	.05	*.00*	.11**	*.02*
Block 2: psychological traits				
Leisure boredom	−.16***		−.18***	
Narcissism				
Superiority	.03		.03	
Exploitativeness	.09*		.10**	
Self-absorption	.01		.03	
Leadership	−.07	*.12*	−.12**	*.14*
Block 3: social traits				
Need for affiliation	.23***		.19***	
Impression management				
Self-promotion	.06		.10**	
Ingratiation	.12**		.08	
Manipulation	.01		−.07*	
Damage control	.04	*.13*	.01	*.11*
Block 4: gratifications-obtained				
Friendship maintenance	.14***		.10**	
Social exchange	−.00		−.06	
Peer attention	.03		.16***	
Free expression	.07*		.07	
Information seeking	.08*		.02	
Identity creation and management	.01		−.02	
Escape	.03	*.03*	.03	*.04*
Block 5: social media use				
IM	.02		.01	
SNS	.01		−.02	
Blog	.04		−.04	
Microblog	.00	*.00*	−.04	*.00*
Block 6: social media addiction				
Preoccupation	−.02		−.05	
Adverse consequences	.04		−.01	
Alleviation of negative emotions	.05		−.00	
Loss of interest in social activities	−.15***	*.02*	−.09*	*.00*
R^2		*.30*		*.31*
Final adjusted R^2		*.29*		*.30*
F	35.20***		26.48***	

Note: ***$p<.001$; **$p<.01$; *$p<.05$. $N=763$ and 709

As shown in Tables 6.4 and 6.5, demographics were entered first into the equations. Results showed that older girls tend to have more bonding social capital ($\beta=.11$, $p<.01$). However, age did not show any effect on bridging social capital

Table 6.5 Hierarchical regressions of demographics, sociopsychological traits, gratifications, level of use, and social media addiction on adolescent bridging social capital

	Bridging social capital—boys		Bridging social capital—girls	
Predictors	β	ΔR^2	β	ΔR^2
Block 1: demographics				
Age	.03	*.00*	.05	*.00*
Block 2: psychological traits				
Leisure boredom	−.12***		−.11**	
Narcissism				
Superiority	−.03		.10**	
Exploitativeness	.09**		.06	
Self-absorption	.07*		.06	
Leadership	−.06*	*.13*	−.12***	*.14*
Block 3: social traits				
Need for affiliation	.35***		.32***	
Impression management				
Self-promotion	−.04		.04	
Ingratiation	.18***		.09*	
Manipulation	.02		−.08*	
Damage control	.04	*.25*	.06	*.18*
Block 4: gratifications-obtained				
Friendship maintenance	.13***		.06	
Social exchange	−.02		.02	
Peer attention	.01		.10**	
Free expression	.02		.12**	
Information seeking	.06		.06	
Identity creation and management	.02		.05	
Escape	.06	*.02*	.04	*.03*
Block 5: social media use				
IM	−.01		.00	
SNS	.02		.02	
Blog	.04		−.03	
Microblog	−.00	*.00*	.02	*.00*
Block 6: social media addiction				
Preoccupation	.03		.01	
Adverse consequences	.01		.04	
Alleviation of negative emotions	.04		.05	
Loss of interest in social activities	−.09**	*.01*	−.12**	*.01*
R^2		*.41*		*.36*
Final adjusted R^2		*.40*		*.35*
F	57.17***		32.47***	

Note: ***$p<.001$; **$p<.01$; *$p<.05$. $N=762$ and 709

for either boys or girls. This demographic block accounted for 0 % and 2 % of the variance for bonding social capital of boys and girls, respectively, but explained none of the variance for bridging social capital.

Psychological traits leisure boredom and narcissism were entered next in the second block. Results revealed that both boys and girls who experienced leisure boredom tended to have less bonding social capital ($\beta = -.16$, $p < .001$, and $\beta = -.18$, $p < .001$, respectively) and less bridging social capital ($\beta = -.12$, $p < .001$, and $\beta = -.11$, $p < .01$, respectively). For narcissism, superiority helped girls gain more bridging social capital ($\beta = .10$, $p < .01$). More exploitative boys had both more bonding and bridging social capital ($\beta = .09$, $p < .05$, and $\beta = .09$, $p < .01$, respectively), while more exploitative girls gained only more bonding social capital ($\beta = .10$, $p < .01$). Self-absorbed boys tended to have more bridging social capital ($\beta = .07$, $p < .05$). Leadership decreased both bonding and bridging social capital of girls ($\beta = -.12$, $p < .01$, and $\beta = -.12$, $p < .001$, respectively) but only lowered the bridging social capital of boys ($\beta = -.06$, $p < .05$). This block accounted for 12 % and 14 % of the total variance for the bonding social capital of boys and girls, respectively, while it explained 13 % and 14 % of the total variance for their bridging social capital, respectively.

Social traits need for affiliation and impression management were entered in the third block. Results showed that both boys and girls who had a strong sense of need for affiliation tended to have both more bonding social capital ($\beta = .23$, $p < .001$, and $\beta = .19$, $p < .001$, respectively) and more bridging social capital ($\beta = .35$, $p < .001$, and $\beta = .32$, $p < .001$, respectively). Girls who were good at self-promotion in social media ($\beta = .10$, $p < .01$) gained more bonding social capital. Ingratiation in social media helped boys gain both more bonding and bridging social capital ($\beta = .12$, $p < .01$, and $\beta = .18$, $p < .001$, respectively), while it only helped girls gain more bridging social capital ($\beta = .09$, $p < .05$). However, manipulation in social media decreased girls' bonding and bridging social capital ($\beta = -.07$, $p < .05$, and $\beta = -.08$, $p < .05$, respectively). This block consisting of social traits accounted for 13 % and 11 % of the total variance for bonding social capital of boys and girls, respectively, while it explained 25 % and 18 % of the total variance for their bridging social capital, respectively.

Social media gratifications-obtained were entered next in the fourth block. Results revealed friendship maintenance in social capital increased both bonding and bridging social capital of boys ($\beta = .14$, $p < .001$, and $\beta = .13$, $p < .001$, respectively), while it only helped girls to gain more bonding social capital ($\beta = .10$, $p < .01$). Girls who used social media for attracting peer attention tended to gain both more bonding and bridging social capital ($\beta = .16$, $p < .001$, and $\beta = .10$, $p < .01$, respectively). Free expression increased boys' bonding social capital ($\beta = .07$, $p < .05$), while it increased girls' bridging social capital ($\beta = .12$, $p < .01$). Furthermore, boys who enjoyed information seeking in social media tended to gain more bonding social capital ($\beta = .08$, $p < .05$). This block of gratifications accounted for 3 % and 4 % of the total variance for bonding social capital of boys and girls, respectively, while it explained 2 % and 3 % of the total variance for their bridging social capital, respectively.

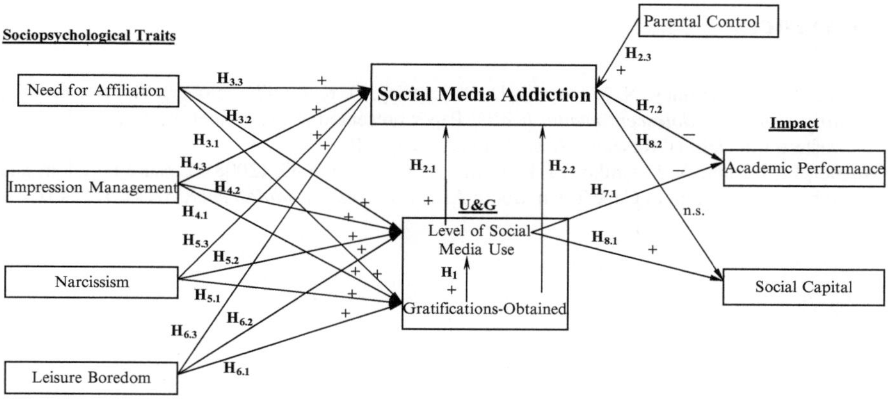

Fig. 6.1 Hypothesis testing results

The level of use in each social medium was entered next in the fifth block. Surprisingly, the use of IM, SNS, blogs, and microblogs did not significantly predict either bonding or bridging social capital of either boys or girls. This block explained none of the total variance. This result indicates that controlling for demographics, sociopsychological traits of adolescents, and the gratifications they obtained from social media, the level of social media use actually had no impact on adolescent social capital.

Finally, social media addiction symptoms were entered in the last block. Results suggested that both boys and girls who lost interest in offline social activities because of social media addiction suffered from decreases of both bonding social capital ($\beta = -.15$, $p < .001$, and $\beta = -.09$, $p < .05$, respectively) and bridging social capital ($\beta = -.09$, $p < .01$, and $\beta = -.12$, $p < .01$, respectively). This block accounted for 2 % and 0 % of the total variance for bonding social capital of boys and girls, respectively, while it explained both 1 % of the total variance for their bridging social capital.

As a whole, all these variables accounted for 29 % and 30 % of the variance for bonding social capital of boys and girls, respectively, and explained 40 % and 35 % of the variance for their bridging social capital, respectively.

To recap, social media addiction indeed has a negative impact on adolescent social capital. If adolescents are addicted to social media and lose interest in offline social activities, both their bonding and bridging social capital will decrease. Although previous research suggested that social media use can increase adolescent social capital, and the correlation results in this study also revealed a positive correlation between adolescent social media use and social capital, the regression results suggest that the social capital of adolescents is actually largely determined by their sociopsychological traits.

Figure 6.1 reveals the hypothesis testing results in this study.

References

Aalsma, M. C., Varshney, N. M., Arens, D., & Lapsley, D. K. (1997, October). *The two faces of narcissism and adolescent mental health.* Paper presented at the annual meeting of the Mid-Western Educational Research Association, Chicago, IL.

Wegner, L., Flisher, A. J., Chikobvu, P., Lombard, C., & King, G. (2008). Leisure boredom and high school dropout in Cape Town, South Africa. *Journal of Adolescence, 31*(3), 421–431.

Chapter 7
Beyond the Survey: What Parents and Teachers Said

The main part of this study is a nationwide survey among adolescents in urban cities, to examine their social media addiction in terms of uses and gratifications, the effects of sociopsychological traits, and impact on academic performance and social capital. To provide an overall picture of social media addiction among adolescents, the viewpoints of both parents and teachers are also very important. Thus, after the analysis of the survey data, 15 parents and 15 teachers of the adolescents who participated in the survey were invited for one-on-one in-depth interviews. Most of the interviewed teachers were in charge of the classes, so they were more familiar with the students' daily behaviors and were responsible for keeping in touch with parents. The parents interviewed were recommended by teachers as those who had concerns and opinions about adolescents' social media addiction and were willing to express them. The topic of "social media addiction among adolescents" easily triggered sharing and complaints from parents and teachers. Most of them were active participants during the interviews, sharing their feelings of frustrations or helplessness. These parent and teacher interviews not only helped to interpret some findings in the survey, but also to uncover the concerns of parents and teachers on adolescents' social media addiction.

In this chapter, qualitative interview data will be categorized and organized to represent parents' and teachers' views on adolescents' social media addiction. Along with the previous findings from the quantitative survey among adolescents, this aims at providing a comprehensive understanding of the status quo of social media addiction among adolescents in urban China.

7.1 Social Media Addiction: At Home

Many teachers complained that some parents did not control their children's social media use at home properly, thus leading to social media addiction among adolescents. At the same time, parents expressed their own difficulties and helplessness in

H. Huang, *Social Media Generation in Urban China: A Study of Social Media Use and Addiction among Adolescents*, Understanding China,
DOI 10.1007/978-3-642-45441-7_7, © Springer-Verlag Berlin Heidelberg 2014

controlling their children's social media use effectively at home. This section discusses inappropriate social media use among adolescents at home, uncovered by parents and teachers.

Zheng, a teacher who was in charge of a Grade 10 class, said that even though some students considered him old-fashioned, he did not encourage them to use social media:

> You never know what those students do with social media. They are much cleverer than you think. I noticed students use QQ to copy each others' homework, you know how? They use webcam through QQ! Sometimes they take pictures of their homework using webcam and send them to each other through QQ, and sometimes they show those homework answers directly through webcam in QQ! How can I be not angry about this?! (Zheng, a teacher in charge of a Grade 10 class)

Some teachers pointed out that parents did not pay enough attention to their children's social media use. Chen, a teacher who was in charge of a Grade 8 class, said she had organized a QQ group in her class, and almost all of the students had joined the group; that way, she could know who was online in QQ. She sometimes found that some students appeared online the whole evening during workdays, and even until very late at night, which meant they might be online the whole evening or they might just keep QQ on in the background while doing their homework. As a teacher, Chen really doubted whether they could concentrate on their homework like that: "Where are their parents?!" she asked.

Li, a teacher who was also in charge of a Grade 8 class, pointed out that some parents were very busy with their own business, so they had the children live with their grandparents or let them stay at home by themselves at night to do their homework. In this kind of situation, some students who were not that self-disciplined would spend lots of time on social media, chatting with friends or even with strangers:

> Adolescence is a crucial period in a person's development. Some parents expect that the school and teachers will be able to provide enough guidance. But we always say that parents are the best teachers for their children. Parents should spend more time with their children! (Li, a teacher in charge of a Grade 8 class)

Several parents expressed frustration when talking about their children's social media use at home. They said they really would like to control their children's social media use, but they don't know how to get involved. Xu, a doctor with a 14-year-old daughter in Grade 8, said that she felt very confused and didn't know how to mediate her daughter's social media use:

> My daughter always shared her thoughts and feelings with me when she was in primary school. I know her QQ password before, and I sometimes checked her friends list or message history, to make sure she hadn't made bad friends. But gradually, especially this year, she has stopped sharing everything with me. I know she is becoming a teenager and would like to be independent. I show my understanding. But she changed her QQ password. She has a blog, too. I encouraged her to write blogs before, because, you know, keeping a diary is a good habit. But now she sets a password for her blog and I cannot get into that, either. I ask her if she can share her blog with me, but she says nothing in particular about that. There is no way for me to know the contents of her blog and her QQ chatting. Her grades are almost as good as before, so I just let it go. But you know, as a mother

of a girl, I definitely don't want her to make bad friends or be bothered by some affairs…. (Xu, mother of a 14-year-old girl)

Wang, the father of a boy who is in Grade 10, also expressed difficulties in controlling his son's social media use:

My son usually does his homework in front of the computer. He says he needs to use PPTs or some course materials uploaded by teachers in the online learning system. I noticed he always kept his QQ on, and sometimes played some small games like Happy Farm in Kaixin or in QQ. When he noticed me walking close to the computer, he would close those things immediately. I told him to close QQ when he was doing his homework, but he said many of his classmates were on and they need to discuss some questions in the homework. Then I bought a printer at home, asking him to print out the PPTs or course materials he needed, and to close the computer when he did his homework. It seemed that the situation was better for a while. But I go on business trips very often, and his mother is much more lenient with him than I am. Now he still does his homework in front of the computer. As parents, we really cannot keep an eye on his screen every minute to see what he is doing…. (Wang, father of a 16-year-old boy)

Zhang, a mother of a girl who is in Grade 9, said she can limit her daughter's social media use during the semesters, but it is impossible to control her use during vacations. She wished that schools could arrange more offline social activities for adolescents in summer or winter vacations:

My husband and I are not teachers, so we need to work when our daughter has her summer or winter vacations. She didn't have many school activities and would stay at home by herself during summer and winter vacations, when her father and I went to work. She might get bored at home, and so she would spend lots of time on social media, such as chatting with friends in QQ or sharing things with friends in Renren. We were not able to control that, since we were both at work during daytime. Thus, we hope the school can arrange more activities for students during vacations. Most adolescents now are the only child at home. They should have more group activities with peers offline, instead of staying at home themselves and interacting with each other in front of a screen. (Zhang, mother of a girl in Grade 9)

When the parents were asked why they thought the survey results showed the stricter the parental control of adolescents' social media use, the more likely they were to be addicted to social media, many parents complained that it is really becoming more and more difficult to control their sons or daughters, as they are not as obedient and dependent on parents as they were before. Adolescents are becoming independent and don't want parents to control them much.

Yao, a mother of a girl in Grade 11, became very angry as she was discussing her daughter's social media use. She said she did control it, but not well, and her daughter could always figure out some way to use them:

My daughter is an active and outgoing girl. She is seventeen this year. She was in another school when she was in Grades 7–9. Last year, when she first entered this high school, I noticed she used QQ a lot to contact her old friends. I thought she might need some time to get involved in the new school, and still needed the friendship or support from her old friends, so I didn't control her use that much. She is in Grade 11 this year. You know, the workload is heavier in Grade 11, and this year is important. I used to limit her time on social media from Monday to Friday. She was allowed 15 minutes every day after she finished her homework and before going to shower. Because the time that she is online is not necessarily

> the same time her friends are online, she now uses QQ less to chat with friends; instead, she uses Sina microblog. She writes something, and when her friends get online, they leave comments. I noticed one boy interacts with her a lot on the microblog. You know, a girl her age always has some secrets, but I don't want her to get distracted. Now I only let her to use the computer on the weekend. However, I noticed that sometimes she would use social media secretly when I went out in the evening, or when I was taking a shower. I noticed twice that even after she told me she had gone to sleep, she used her mobile phone to update her microblog secretly on her bed! I was very angry... Now I ask her to put her mobile phone in the living room when she goes to bed.... (Yao, mother of a 17-year-old girl)

Li is the mother of a 16-year-old boy who is now in Grade 10. She said her boy loved "Transformers" and collected them since he was young. But since he joined an SNS group formed by fans of Transformers, he has been very interested in uploading pictures of his collections and discussing with others. Because the boy had many special collections, he always received admiration from other fans and participated a lot in SNS group discussion. Li had no idea how to control her son's SNS use, except moving the computer out of study room into the living room. But then the boy used the mobile phone to get online for SNS group. Li noticed it from the high data traffic and her son's mobile phone bill. Li then took away her son's smartphone and gave him a very simple mobile phone that could not connect to the Internet.

The above cases indicate parents indeed try to control adolescents' social media use, but adolescents always have various kinds of countermeasures against parents' control. This further confirmed the survey results that the more strictly parents control adolescents' social media use, the more likely they are to be addicted to social media, thus making the parental control even more severe. Adolescence is a rebellious and sensitive age. Tao et al. (2007) pointed out that authoritarian, indulgent, and neglectful parenting styles were all possibly linked to Internet addiction, while an authoritative parenting style could be effective in preventing adolescents from Internet addiction. Therefore, parents should not be forceful in controlling their children's social media use. Instead, they should try to guide their children's social media use to be proper and healthy.

7.2 Social Media Addiction: At School

Adolescents do not only use social media at home; they also use them at school. According to the teachers interviewed, in most middle schools, the computer rooms are only open to students for computer classes. In other schools, although the computer rooms are open to students during extracurricular activities time, the websites they can browse are limited. Some computer rooms also control the time students using the computer: students need their student ID cards to log into the computer, and the system will automatically shut down after 20 min and will not allow the same student to log in again on the same day. The schools have strict control over students' Internet use over school computers, but students have another tool to get online: their mobile phones, which have become a major tool for students to use social media at school.

Fu, a teacher in charge of a Grade 8 class, also organized a QQ group for her class. She said she had noticed some students using QQ through their mobile phones during class time:

> Several times, when I did not have classes and got online in my office, I noticed that a certain student's QQ appeared as mobile QQ online, and it was during class time! Then, during my class, I paid special attention to that student and, indeed, I found him sometimes using his mobile phone during class. Some students are very proficient at using their mobile phones now. It is incredible! They can look at the teacher and pretend they are listening in class, but secretly they are thumbing on their mobile phones to send out messages under the desk! The teachers cannot even notice that! I don't think the QQ use in class is for any special reason; some students just cannot concentrate in class or feel bored, so they use QQ just to kill time…. (Fu, a teacher in charge of a Grade 8 class)

Zheng, the Grade 10 teacher mentioned above, said he was very angry to notice students sending homework answers through QQ at home. He also got very angry that some students used QQ through mobile phones to transmit quizzes at school:

> Students have quizzes from time to time, and one class may take certain quiz earlier than other classes. I noticed that some students took pictures of their quizzes using their mobile phones and sent them to their friends in other classes through mobile QQ. Then, if other classes have the quiz earlier next time, their friends will send the quiz to them in return! Every time I found students using mobile phones in class, I took their phones away from them and asked their parents to come and take the mobile phones back. (Zheng, a teacher of a Grade 10 class)

Teachers said that schools advised parents not to buy mobile phones for their children. However, many parents still buy mobile phones for them in order to stay in touch with them. Some schools' regulations prohibit students from opening their mobile phones once they enter the school gates. If students are caught using mobile phones in class, teachers will take the mobile phones from them, and notices will be sent out to their parents asking them to come and get the mobile phones back. Zheng said that at his school, the policy is that the first time the student is caught, the teacher will keep the phone for 1 week; the second time that student is caught, the teacher will keep it for a month; and if the student is caught for the third time, the teacher will keep it until the end of the semester, at which point the parents can come and get the mobile phone back. It seems that the regulations are strict, but some teachers said it is actually difficult to implement:

> Some students say it is their parents who ask them to take the mobile phones with them to school. I can understand this, because some parents would like to be able to contact their children after school. Some parents also try to limit the students' mobile phone use by controlling the bill. This doesn't work at all! Students said the lowest Internet service package for mobile phones is five *yuan* per month, and the amount of data is more than enough for unlimited use of mobile phone QQ. So, students do not send SMS to each other that often because it is more expensive; instead, they use mobile phone QQ. I even noticed in my class' QQ group, some students' QQ showed "mobile online" 24 hours a day! Parents could not tell this from the phone bill… I also have come across some parents who were not really cooperative. I once noticed a certain student using his mobile phone during class, so I took away the mobile phone from him and asked his parents to come and get it. His parents didn't come, and later I noticed that student had a new mobile phone…. If the parents are

> not cooperative, how can we control students' behavior effectively at school? (Liu, a teacher in charge of a Grade 9 class)

Xia, a Grade 7 teacher, said personally he didn't advise that parents buy mobile phones for students. In the parents' meeting at school, he also told the parents that because Grade 7 students were too young to be self-disciplined, if the parents really wanted to buy mobile phones for their children, it would be best to choose phones without an Internet connection function. Nonetheless, some children still have smartphones or even iPhones. Xia also called for more parental responsibility in guiding students' proper use of social media.

In Tian's school, there are student weekday boarders. She explained:

> Our school has relatively strict rules. The dorms are required to turn out the lights after 11 pm, and electricity is also cut off in each dorm. However, it was noticed that some students still used their mobile phones in bed. To prevent from being noticed due to the light from the phones, they would hide them under the quilts. It is really difficult to control! Some students would fall in puppy love and would chat with their girlfriends or boyfriends through mobile QQ. Some girls would exchange romance novels, and I even noticed that some boys would transmit pornography to each other through their mobile QQ! This really harms them, not only in their studies, but also in their personal development. What we teachers can do is to keep the mobile phone for the students and talk to their parents. As a teacher, I sincerely request parents' attention to this problem…. (Tian, a teacher in charge of a Grade 11 class)

Chen, a teacher in charge of a Grade 8 class, said that in her school, each classroom is equipped with a computer for teaching purposes, which used to be connected to the Internet. Some students used it to get online after class for a while. Last year, when the SNS game Happy Farm was very popular, students even took turns during class breaks to get on SNS to "steal vegetables," which angered the teachers. Then, to make the students concentrate on their studies inside the classroom, the school disconnected the Internet service in each classroom. Chen said schools did make some efforts to control students' social media use. According to a Grade 8 teacher Li, some teachers even suggested to the school authorities to shield mobile phone services signals in classroom areas so that students would not be distracted by mobile phone or social media use at school, especially during class time.

The interviews revealed that, on the one hand, some teachers were not satisfied with parental control over adolescents' social media use, but on the other hand, some parents complained about feeling helpless in being able to effectively mediate their children's social media use. It is suggested that parents and teachers cooperate with each other more in order to cope with adolescents' social media addiction.

7.3 Impact of Social Media on Adolescents' Academic Performance

When asked about the impact of social media on adolescents' academic performance, some parents and teachers were pessimistic, saying that social media use would definitely occupy the adolescents' study time and distract them, thereby impairing their academic performance. However, other parents and teachers were optimistic, suggesting that if adolescents used social media to discuss questions and share useful information, or to relax and entertain themselves to properly refresh their minds, social media use may benefit their academic performance. Other parents' opinions were more neutral.

7.3.1 Pessimistic Views

The pessimistic perspective holding by parents and teachers can be further categorized into the following four kinds of views:

View 1: Social media can distract adolescents from their studies. Some teachers, especially high school teachers, thought the main duty of the adolescents was to study. These teachers suggest that adolescents have as few distractions as possible so that they can concentrate on their study: "If students do their homework while their QQ is on-screen, how can they concentrate on their homework?" Some parents also admitted that they themselves sometimes could not help chatting with others through MSN or kept checking information in SNS while working: "We adults sometimes cannot control ourselves, so how can the adolescents be self-disciplined enough?"

View 2: The misuse of social media at the wrong time for the wrong purposes will harm adolescents' studies. As mentioned above, some teachers found students transmitting homework answers or even quizzes through QQ. Some students use mobile QQ during class time or even keep mobile QQ on 24 h a day. Such misuse will definitely impair their academic performance.

View 3: Some students face difficulties in school learning or are lacking a sense of achievement in their studies, so they turn to social media for a sense of achievement and to temporarily forget their academic troubles. Teachers and parents suggested that some students who did not perform well in their studies and did not often receive praise from teachers and parents would turn to social media to show off in some other aspects, to get admiration from others. For example, some adolescents showed off their collections or special knowledge on cars or Transformers in related SNS groups. Although actively seeking a sense of achievement can be good for students' psychological well-being, the excessive use of social media to escape from academic responsibilities can harm their academic performance.

View 4: Social media can facilitate puppy love among adolescents, which can negatively affect their academic performance. Social media indeed provides more chances for adolescents to stay in touch with their peers. However, as mentioned above, some misuse of social media after lights out among boys and girls would make adolescents sleep later at night and feel tired in class the next day, thus affecting their school performance.

7.3.2 Optimistic Views

Despite the above possible negative impact, some parents and teachers still insisted that, if used properly, social media can help to improve adolescents' academic performance.

View 1: Class QQ groups help to share course materials and facilitate discussions after class, which can be useful for adolescents' studies. Many teachers said they had organized QQ groups in their classes, where they then uploaded PPTs and other course materials. Some students also discussed or debated questions in the QQ groups, and the discussions could be seen by other members in the group and inspire further participation. All these are beneficial to students' academic performance.

View 2: Adolescents can seek and share useful information in social media, which can also benefit their learning. Wang said his son was interested in international relations and often read the blogs of commentators, which could help him gain more insights into current international relations. In another example, Deng said her son was interested in chemistry experiments and joined an SNS group called "chemistry changes the world." He read to find out about experiments others did and to try them out himself, and he also posted some results of his experiments to share with others. Deng was very proud that her son won the second prize in the Chemistry Olympiad Exams of Guangzhou last year and said that the exchange of knowledge in social media can help adolescents inspire each other to learn, which was beneficial. In yet another example, Chen said that her daughter was preparing to take the TOEFL and sometimes discussed her progress through QQ groups with other students she met in an English training course. They not only shared information, but also encouraged each other. Chen also believed these positive discussions could benefit their studies.

7.3.3 Neutral Views

Although many parents and teachers pointed out several possible positive or negative impact of social media use on adolescents' academic performance, some parents and teachers held more neutral viewpoints. They pointed out that, if used properly, social media use would not affect adolescents' academic performance, but they also did not believe social media could effectively improve adolescents' academic performance: "I can only say that, if adolescents use social media for a reasonable amount of time and with healthy contents, their academic performance should not be affected. But I rarely see the case that student's academic performance is largely improved because he or she uses social media a lot," said Xia, a teacher in charge of a Grade 7 class.

7.4 Impact of Social Media on Adolescents' Social Capital

Parents and teachers were also asked about the impact of social media on adolescents' social capital, and again their views can be divided into optimistic, pessimistic, and neutral. Parents and teachers who held optimistic views thought social media were not only communication tools for adolescents to keep in touch with friends, but also new platforms for them to demonstrate their expertise and specialties. However, those who held pessimistic views pointed out that social media may occupy much of the adolescents' leisure time and thus reduce their offline social activities with friends, thereby decreasing their social capital. Meanwhile, there were also parents and teachers with more neutral views.

7.4.1 Optimistic Views

Social media provides opportunities for teachers and parents to understand more about the adolescents' thoughts and inner feelings, which helps adolescents to gain more bonding social capital. Fu, a Grade 8 teacher, said that because most of the students in her class had joined the class QQ group, she could visit students' QQ spaces (blog service provided by QQ) if they had them and they were open to friends. She thought that social media not only provided spaces for adolescents to present themselves, but also provided a new angle from which teachers and parents could know more about the adolescents. Teachers and parents can find out about the interest and current thoughts of adolescents through social media, so as to communicate with them more effectively. Fu said she always left comments on students' QQ spaces to praise or to encourage them. If she found a certain student expressing troubles or confusion in the space, she would also try to chat with him or her to help out. By getting more attention from teachers and parents, adolescents are able to gain more bonding social capital from social media use.

Information sharing through social media can help adolescents to gain more bridging social capital. Most Chinese adolescents are the only child at home, and they are not used to sharing things with others. Some parents and teachers suggested that social media helped adolescents learn to share things with others and at the same time, respect and respond to others' sharing. They share learning materials, personal interest, personal collections, dairies, and photos with others and also receive others' comments, praise, and encouragement in return. For example, Deng's son learned about others' chemistry experiments through the SNS group and also shared his experiments with others, and Chen's daughter exchanged TOEFL materials with peers through QQ. These kinds of sharing can indeed help increase adolescents' bridging social capital.

7.4.2 Pessimistic Views

Although there were many reasonable optimistic possibilities, some parents and teachers still insisted that social media use could occupy too much of adolescents' leisure time and reduce their offline social activities with relatives and friends, thus possibly decreasing their social capital. Yao, mother of a girl in Grade 11 mentioned above, said her daughter used to hang out with her cousins on weekends. Because she now spends much of her time on social media contacting her pervious friends in junior middle school, when her cousins called her out, she always had many reasons to refuse. After several times, her cousins thought she did not like to hang out with them and stopped asking her to go out: "I am a bit worried, since now at family gatherings, she and her cousins are not as close as they were before," Yao said. Some teachers also pointed out that if adolescents use social media by sacrificing the time they go out offline with friends, their social capital may decrease. They also suggested that since adolescents already spend a lot of time studying, if they have leisure time, they should go out with friends instead of staying in front of a screen.

7.4.3 Neutral Views

There were also some parents and teachers who felt more neutral about the impact of social media on adolescents' social capital. They thought that proper use would not decrease adolescents' social capital, but since communication through social media was essentially virtual, it might not help increase their social capital either. Wu, a lawyer and also the mother of a girl in Grade 10, said she believed relationships based on face-to-face communication were much more solid than relationships built through online communication: "Although I do not limit my daughter's social media use, I do not want her to get used to communicating with others virtually, either. I always encourage her to go out for hobby groups or summer camps to meet more friends face-to-face. I don't think substantial social capital is built in virtual spaces, but rather it is based on mutual understanding in the real world," Wu said.

Tian, a teacher in charge of a Grade 11 class, viewed the impact from another perspective. She said that if adolescents spent much time on social media for communicating with others, their online social capital might be increased, but at the same time, since their leisure time was limited, their time participating in offline social activities with friends offline would have to be reduced, and thus their offline social capital could possibly be decreased. As a result, it is difficult to tell exactly whether adolescents' social capital is increased or decreased through social media use.

Through the above interviews, parents and teachers expressed their concerns about social media addiction among adolescents. As supplements to the quantitative data, these interviews provide a lively and concrete depiction of problematic social media use among adolescents in daily life from the viewpoint of parents and teachers. Along with the survey results presented previously, the findings of this study reveal that social media addiction is indeed now a problem among adolescents in urban China with which parents and educators should take action to cope.

Reference

Tao, R., Ying, L., Yue, X., & Hao, X. (2007). *Internet addiction: Exploration and interventions*. Shanghai: Century Publishing Group.

Chapter 8
Discussion and Conclusions

Adolescents today are technologically savvy and heavily immersed in social media, which provide more channels and possibilities for them to stay in touch with friends. They chat with friends through IM; they use SNS to connect and maintain their social networks; and they share their lives intensively through blogs and instantly through microblogs. They may even prefer socializing with friends via social media to going out with them offline. Many policymakers and critics have voiced fears about what the effect of communication technologies on adolescents' lives.

This exploratory research proposes the concept of social media addiction and is the first to test empirically and report on the social media addiction phenomenon among adolescents in urban China. It adopts the uses and gratifications (U&G) approach and aims at identifying the social and psychological origins of the needs, which generate expectations regarding social media and lead to differential patterns of social media use, resulting in need gratification and/or social media addiction and possible consequences for academic performance and social capital. Previous addiction research usually focused on level of addiction or on treating addiction as a dichotomous variable. However, this study further identifies four social media addiction symptoms that can help parents and teachers to detect the addiction in adolescents in order to provide them with proper intervention at an early stage.

This chapter provides an overall picture of the phenomenon of social media addiction among adolescents in urban China. Social media addiction is discussed in terms of the severity, addiction symptoms, sociopsychological antecedents, gratifications-obtained, impact, and coping strategies. Theoretical and practical implications of this study are also elaborated. Finally, the limitations of the study are addressed before suggestions for future research are provided.

H. Huang, *Social Media Generation in Urban China: A Study of Social Media Use and Addiction among Adolescents*, Understanding China,
DOI 10.1007/978-3-642-45441-7_8,

8.1 Social Media Addiction Among Adolescents in Urban China

8.1.1 Severity of Social Media Addiction

Using the classic definition of Internet addiction by Young (1999), 15.6 % of the adolescents in this sample were classified as social media addicts. Using the Internet population figures reported by CNNIC (2011), it can be estimated that as many as 20 million adolescents in China might be addicted. According to the findings, they spent around 3 h daily actively engaging in social media. Compared with nonaddicts, these addicted adolescents spent more time on IM, SNS, blogs, and microblogs every day. They had more friends and more frequent contact friends in social media than nonaddicts.

These findings indicate that social media addiction cannot be taken lightly now. In the past, parents and educators have paid much attention to prevent adolescents from game addiction, but they may have overlooked their social media use, because they might have overvalued how social media can help to maintain or facilitate adolescents' interpersonal networks. This study demonstrates that, although it may not be as severe as online game addiction, social media addiction indeed exists among adolescents. It presents a new challenge to which parents and educators should pay close attention.

The intensity of social media use is an indicator of social media addiction. If adolescents spend excessive amounts of time on social media to communicate with others, they may show a high tendency to addiction. Parents should pay attention not only to adolescents' time online through computers but also to their time on mobile phones, especially 3G phones, as 20 % of the respondents indicated that they used mobile phones more frequently than computers to go online.

Because a phenomenal increase in the social media use is predicted for the coming year (CNNIC 2011), social media addiction may affect more people in the near future. It may exist among not only adolescents but also various age groups, such as among college students and white-collar workers. Previous research suggested that excessive online communication could make people alienated, isolated, and desocialized, in addition to causing interpersonal communication disturbances such as social phobia or social anxiety (Li et al. 2009; Wang and Yu 2006; Zhang and Hu 2010). Thus, social media addiction as a social phenomenon can no longer be neglected. Social media have already changed the way we create and use content (Comm 2010), and now social media addiction is becoming a social problem that calls for public attention.

8.1.2 Social Media Addiction Symptoms

Past Internet addiction research among Chinese adolescents usually focused on identifying the extent or severity of addiction in the study sample (Cao and Su 2007;

Geng et al. 2006; Gong et al. 2009; Li et al. 2006; Liu 2007; Yang and Tung 2007). In addition to the severity of addiction, this study further identified four social media addiction symptoms in adolescents. *Preoccupation* indicates that adolescents are preoccupied by social media and have a strong desire for them, and social media use is the dominant activity in their leisure time. *Adverse consequences* reveals that adolescents suffer from negative consequences because of excessive social media use such as school performance or productivity impairments, but they still continue to use them. *Alleviation of negative emotions* suggests that adolescents use social media to relieve dysphoric moods or escape from disturbing thoughts. *Loss of interest in social activities* refers to the preference of adolescents to social media rather than going out offline for social activities with friends. These addiction symptoms reveal the multifactorial nature of social media addiction, and each symptom demonstrates an array of domains of behavioral consequences of adolescents' social media addiction.

Although intensity of social media use is an important indicator for addiction, it may not be sufficient. This study suggests that addiction symptoms provide additional and valuable indicators for parents and educators to detect adolescents' social media addiction. If students appear to be preoccupied by social media, constantly alleviate negative emotions through social media, suffer from adverse consequences, and lose interest in offline social activities because of social media use, they are very likely to be addicted to social media. Few studies have focused on social media addiction symptoms as a supplementary assessment to identify addicts. This study reveals that symptoms are signals calling for proper interventions and guidance for adolescents' social media behaviors.

These social media addiction symptoms are consistent with many of the symptoms proposed by DSM-IV for identifying substance dependence, that is, "preoccupation with the substance, loss of control over the substance, withdrawal, tolerance, more use of the substance than intended, continued consumption of the substance despite adverse consequences, and loss of interest in other social, occupational, and recreational activities" (APA 1994). However, not all symptoms were found in this study, which may be because behavioral dependence is different from substance dependence or some items were deleted in the factor analysis to achieve a stable factor structure. Future research can identify additional addiction symptoms to provide earlier warning signs for parents and educators to devise treatments and prevention programs.

8.1.3 Sociopsychological Antecedents of Social Media Addiction

This study reveals that adolescents with certain sociopsychological traits are more likely to be addicted to social media. Parents and teachers should pay attention to adolescents with certain sociopsychological traits, especially if they are heavy users of social media, and provide guidance to prevent them from becoming addicted.

This study found that adolescents who were leisurely bored were more likely to be addicted to social media and suffer from various symptoms. Discriminant analysis showed that leisure boredom was also an important criterion to distinguish social media addicts from nonaddicts. This finding is in line with previous findings that those who are bored in leisure tend to be addicted to the Internet (Lin et al. 2009) and mobile phone (Leung 2008). When available leisure experiences are not sufficiently frequent, involving, or exciting, leisure boredom is likely to result (Iso-Ahola and Weissinger 1990). According to Lin and Yu (2008), avoiding boredom is one of the major motivations for Internet use. Increasingly, social media allow adolescents, while having nothing to do, to be engaged in various online activities such as text chatting or video chatting with friends in IM, sharing photos in SNS, updating blogs, and reading others' blogs or microblogs. As a result, providing diverse offline social activities as supplements and alternatives to adolescents who are bored in their leisure time may be an effective way to prevent them from social media addiction.

Self-absorption is one of the characteristics of a narcissistic personality. Adolescents who are self-absorbed enjoy bragging to others about the good things they have done and being told that they have done a good job; they like to look at themselves in the mirror often. These adolescents may not only enjoy others' praise offline but also indulge in being complimented by others online through social media. Thus, they are prone to be addicted to social media. This finding is in accordance with Twenge and Campbell (2009) that narcissism reveals a very positive and inflated sense of self, which is demonstrated by a preoccupation with MySpace, Facebook, and YouTube to show off and be complimented by others. If parents and teachers notice adolescents who are self-absorbed and overindulge heavily in social media, they should provide guidance to them.

Unlike self-absorption, other dimensions of narcissism are not likely to lead to addiction. For example, superiority is a characteristic of someone who considers himself or herself a great or special person. Exploitativeness is revealed in someone who believes he or she can control other people easily; and leadership is demonstrated in someone who always wants to be the leader. These narcissistic personalities are not likely to explain social media addiction, probably because online communication places more emphasis on mutual respect (Hindman 2007), and the interaction in social media features reciprocity, as revealed in this study. These may not satisfy the needs of adolescents who are superior, exploitative, and have a strong sense of leadership. Therefore, these adolescents are not likely to become addicted.

Some adolescents are more competent than others in impression management tactics. Those who are good at online impression management have full control over their published information, so their online self-presentation can be more strategic (Kramer and Winter 2008) and based on longer and more systematic considerations than in face-to-face self-presentation (Leary 1996). The present study identified that adolescents usually use four impression management tactics in social media: they demonstrate positive accomplishments in social media for *self-promotion*; they compliment others in social media so that others consider them friendly through *ingratiation*; they make excuses in social media for not getting good grades or depreciate rivals through *manipulation*; and they apologize or justify their behaviors to reduce negative impressions of others in social media for *damage control*. Discriminant analysis showed that adolescent social media addicts were indeed better at impression management tactics than nonaddicts. Furthermore, this study also demonstrates that adolescents who excel at manipulation in social media are likely to get addicted. That is, in a vicious circle, adolescents who always excuse themselves for not getting good grades or being blamed by others tend to be addicted to social media, so they repeatedly get bad grades and are blamed by others. Therefore, if adolescents do not achieve good academic results, parents and teachers should not blindly blame them, but patiently help them to find reasons and solutions and constantly encourage them. Otherwise, adolescents will turn to social media to offer excuses for themselves. Compared with manipulation, other impression management tactics do not have obvious harmful effects and do not form vicious circles. In addition, this study also reveals that tactics such as self-promotion and ingratiation may even help adolescents to increase their social capital. Therefore, they are not likely to lead to addiction.

The need for affiliation can be seen as a tendency to receive social gratifications from harmonious relationships (Murray 1938). It is revealed that adolescents who have a strong need for affiliation are able to use social media properly. Regression results suggest that adolescents who have a strong need for affiliation are not likely to be addicted to social media or lose interest in offline social activities. Indeed, they may prefer offline social activities to online interaction because offline social activities can provide them with a strong sense of belonging to social groups in the real world.

Previous Internet addiction research usually investigated psychological antecedents of the addiction such as shyness (Chak and Leung 2004; Huang and Leung 2009; Yuen and Lavin 2004), loneliness (Ghassemzadeh et al. 2008; Nalwa and Anand 2003; Odaci and Kalkan; 2010), alienation (Huang and Leung 2009), self-esteem (Ghassemzadeh et al. 2008; Ko et al. 2007), and depression (Cheung and Wong 2011; Tsai and Lin 2003). To emphasize the social features of social media, this study further explores the social antecedents that possibly trigger social media addiction. Based on the previous literature and suggested by the focus group results, this study selected two social traits (i.e., need for affiliation and impression management) and two psychological traits (i.e., narcissism and leisure boredom) to test whether they were the antecedents of social media addiction. Results supported such proposition, and social traits and psychological traits indeed formed two most powerful blocks, with each explaining 11 % of the variance for social media addiction. This indicates that social traits are as important as psychological traits for predicting social media addiction, and adolescents with certain traits are prone to be addicted. Sociopsychological traits are either inherent or shaped by the environment and thus are difficult to change. Parents and teachers should pay close attention to adolescents with certain personality traits and direct their social media usage properly. Moreover, future research can test other traits such as procrastination and affinity seeking, which are also possible antecedents of adolescents' social media addiction.

8.1.4 Gratifications and Social Media Addiction

In addition to sociopsychological traits, the study shows that indulging in gratifications obtained from social media can also lead to addiction. The distinctive features of social media provide adolescents with seven kinds of gratifications: adolescents can keep in touch and maintain relationships with friends through social media for *friendship maintenance*; they enjoy *social exchange* from the reciprocity of online exchange for comments and virtual gifts in social media; they make efforts to attract comments and feedback from friends via social media for *peer attention*; they enjoy the unlimited communication in social media for *free expression*; they gain useful information and know current hot topics from social media through *information seeking*; they try out different online identities and demonstrate an ideal self through social media for *identity creation and management*; and they use social media to *escape* from their problems and worries. It is noteworthy that apart from social functions, social media have become one of the major news sources for many users. They discuss via social media topics that are censored by the central government in mass media and rely on them to get news, particularly breaking news or gossip.

Past U&G findings in social media use are diverse and fragmented. The seven social media gratifications identified in this study consolidate previous U&G findings on IM (Cheuk and Chan 2007; Ljungstrand and Segestad 2000; Huang 2008; Hwang 2009; Leung 2001; Quan-Haase and Young 2010; Ramirez et al. 2008; Recchiuti 2003), SNS (Cheung et al. 2011; Dunne and Lawlor 2010; Park et al. 2009; Raacke and Bonds-Raacke 2008; Urista et al. 2009), blogs (Huang et al. 2008; Jung et al. 2007; Lee et al. 2008; Leung 2009; Trammell et al. 2004; Wang and Fesenmaier 2004), and microblogs (Chen 2011; Johnson and Yang 2009; Martinez 2009) and provide an integrated understanding of social media gratifications as a whole. This study also supplements the gratification inventory by adding new dimensions. Social exchange is a new gratification unique to social media. It borrows the idea from social exchange theory (Homans 1958) and reveals the reciprocity obligation in social media interaction. It empathizes that, on one hand, users feel obligated to give their attention in return for the attention they have received from others in social media. On the other hand, they expect to gain an equal amount of attention from their friends after providing their own. Social media expand the norm of reciprocity from offline communication to online interaction. This social exchange gratification highlights the distinct social feature of social media.

The above seven social media gratifications can be further categorized as social, information, and entertainment gratifications, which is in line with the findings of Leung (2009) that the gratifications of user-generated contents on the Internet satisfy social and recognition needs, cognitive needs, and entertainment needs.

Previous research suggested that the gratifications of Internet use played an important antecedent role in explaining Internet dependency (Sun et al. 2006). Since social media gratifications can largely satisfy certain needs of adolescents, it is certain that they also have the potential to lead to addiction. For example, in agreement with the previous literature (Elliott et al. 1996; Tao et al. 2007), this study shows that if adolescents use social media for escaping from problems and worries, it is most likely that they will be addicted to social media, while information seeking through social media is not likely to lead to addiction. Among social, information, and entertainment gratifications, entertainment gratifications were the most powerful predictor of social media addiction, while information gratifications were the least likely to lead to addiction. This finding is in line with previous findings that diversion strongly predicted Internet addiction, while information seeking negatively explained Internet addiction (Song et al. 2004). Therefore, whether or not a certain gratification leads to addiction actually depends on what kind of psychological need it satisfies. If the need is positive and is satisfied by proper use, it may be beneficial, such as information seeking for adolescents through social media. However, if the need is prone to negative consequences and requires an increasing amount of use for satisfaction, it is likely to lead to addiction, such as escape.

Suggested by the hierarchical regression results, this study further investigated relationships among sociopsychological traits, gratifications, and social media addiction. The results revealed the mediation role of gratifications between sociopsychological traits and social media addiction, with social gratifications having more powerful mediating effects than information and entertainment gratifications. This further clarifies the relationship between sociopsychological traits and social media addiction by suggesting that certain personality traits may not necessarily and directly lead to addiction. Addiction ensues only if social media can largely satisfy the needs of people with certain traits by providing sufficient social, entertainment, and information gratifications.

8.1.5 Social Media Addiction, Academic Performance, and Social Capital

Academic performance and social capital are two major concerns of adolescents. Academic performance largely determines their future path, such as what kind of universities they can enter; and social capital implies the quality of their interpersonal relationships. Therefore, this study examined the impact of social media addiction on adolescents focusing on these two important aspects of adolescents, which are also concerns of parents and teachers.

8.1.5.1 Impact on Academic Performance

This study revealed that social media addiction has a negative impact on the academic performance of adolescents. Possible hints for academic performance impairments could be the first thing they do after returning home from school is to turn on the computer and log in to social media accounts; they spend a large amount of time on social media; they often use social media before doing their homework; and they neglect their study tasks to spend more time on social media.

IM is the most widely used social medium among adolescents in urban China; over 90 % of respondents indicated that they have used it. This study reveals that excessive IM use can largely impair adolescents' academic performance. This reinforces the previous findings of Huang and Leung (2009) in their IM addiction study. In in-depth interviews, parents and teachers revealed that adolescents used QQ to transmit homework answers or quiz answers, and they secretly used mobile QQ via mobile phones in class or late at night. These behaviors are likely to have negative effects by reducing the efforts that these adolescents put into study. Therefore, to prevent negative impact on academic performance, parents and teachers should control the IM use of adolescents, via both computers and mobile phones.

In contrast, although addiction will have negative effects on adolescents' academic performance, proper social media use might possibly improve their study. For example, this study demonstrates that SNS use for boys, particularly in friendship maintenance, may facilitate group discussions which can help boys improve their academic results. Meanwhile, information seeking in social media can be encouraged for girls because it can also benefit their study. These differences between boys and girls are probably because boys tend to stay alone and study independently; if they use social media for cooperative learning, it may be helpful for their academic learning; on the contrary, girls enjoy staying together and sharing gossips; if they use social media more for information seeking, it can be useful for their study.

8.1.5.2 Impact on Social Capital

It is usually taken for granted that social media use can increase adolescents' social capital, and thus parents may have relatively lost control over adolescents' social media use. Previous research also suggested that the social media, especially SNS and blogs, can help to increase users' social capital (Cohen 2007; Ellison et al. 2007, 2009; Kerr 2009; Ko and Kuo 2009; Steinfield et al. 2008, 2009). However, this study demonstrates another point of view. The level of social media use per se does not actually increase both bonding and bridging social capital of adolescents. On the contrary, if adolescents are addicted to social media and lose interest in offline social activities, their bonding and bridging social capital will largely decrease. A major reason this study holds a different position from the previous research is that it not only examined the relationships between adolescents' social capital and their social media use but also took into account the sociopsychological traits of adolescents. The study revealed that adolescents' social capital is affected slightly by their social media use but largely depends on their sociopsychological traits. For example, adolescents who have a strong need for affiliation are likely to have more social capital, while those who experience leisure boredom tend to have less social capital.

Although social media addiction decreases the social capital of adolescents, if used properly, certain social media functions can help to increase their social capital. For example, this study revealed that friendship maintenance through social media indeed helps adolescents to increase their social capital. It is interesting to note that information gratifications help boys to accumulate bonding social capital, probably because the relationships between males are often based on or initiated by sharing useful information with each other both online and offline (Lu et al. 2010). On the contrary, girls care more about peer attention, which can help them to increase both bonding and bridging social capital.

Therefore, whether or not social media can increase adolescents' social capital depends not on the level of use per se, but lies in what they use social media for. If adolescents are not addicted to social media and do not lose interest in offline social activities, but make good use of social media for friendship maintenance, peer attention, and information seeking, their social capital can be increased by social media use.

8.1.6 Coping with Adolescents' Social Media Addiction

As described above, social media addiction is now a problem existing among adolescents in urban China and has negative impact on their academic performance and social capital. As a rapid increase of social media users is predicted, addiction may become an even more severe problem in the near future. Social media addiction is a new challenge for parents and educators. How then should we cope with it?

Actually, social media addiction is not only a behavioral dependence. More importantly, it is a signal calling for parents and teachers to pay attention to the psychological well-being of adolescents. Simple limitations on social media use may not be an effective way to solve the problem. Psychologists pointed out that addiction usually indicates that people face severe problems that they cannot overcome and urgently need a channel to relieve them (Wu 2007). If the pressures are not released through heavy usage of social media, they may even lead to other more severe behaviors such as violence or even suicide (Zhao 2010). This study also showed that adolescents are very likely to be addicted to social media if they use social media mainly for escaping from their problems and worries. Thus, there must be some reasons behind adolescents' social media addiction, and the excessive social media use is a way for them to relieve their pressures or psychological problems. Therefore, to cope with adolescents' social media addiction, it is important to examine the origin of these pressures.

Due to the one-child policy, most adolescents in urban China are the only child at home. Consequently, the family members place high expectations on them. These adolescents face all kinds of competition since young childhood. The competition becomes even more severe when they enter middle school because after the 9-year compulsory education, they have to compete with each other for acceptance into high schools and universities. Adolescence is a sensitive period. Adolescents want to be dependent, but at the same time, they strive for recognition from others. If they do not perform well in their studies and are often blamed by parents and teachers, they will be frustrated and under great pressure. It is then likely that these adolescents turn to social media to escape from worries, anxieties, and predicaments and to seek recognition and companionship. Therefore, to cope with adolescents' social media addiction, the key is to eliminate the psychological pressures that might have led them to addiction and provide them with warm and a harmonious environment and companionship offline. Society should be more tolerant of adolescents, especially those who do not perform well at school. Adolescents should not be judged only by their academic performance. A more comprehensive evaluation system needs to be set up to assess adolescents' overall abilities (Tao et al. 2007; Zhao 2010). This may enable adolescents to recognize their strengths and potential, which can help them build self-confidence and thus prevent them from seeking recognition in a virtual world through social media.

8.2 Implications

8.2.1 Theoretical Implications

First, this study enriches the literature of media addiction research. In particular, it contributes to the Internet addiction literature. In China today, Internet addiction, as a "severe social problem that could threaten the nation's future" (Fallows 2007), attracts much attention from parents, educators, health workers, and researchers. A great deal of research on Internet addiction among Chinese adolescents has been conducted in recent years (Cao and Su 2007; Chak and Leung 2004; Cheung and Wong 2011; Geng et al. 2006; Gong et al. 2009; Ko et al. 2007, 2008; Lam et al. 2009; Li et al. 2006; Liu 2007; Tsai and Lin 2003; Yang and Tung 2007). However, almost all of these studies either discussed Internet addiction as a general phenomenon or focused on online game addiction among adolescents, but largely ignoring another possible cause of Internet addiction—online interpersonal communication. As IM, SNS, blogs, and microblogs are increasingly popular among adolescents in urban China, these social media have become so attractive that they make many adolescents indulge in online interpersonal communication. Thus far, almost no study has focused on whether social media use is addictive or dependence forming. This study contributes to the literature by proposing the concept of "social media addiction," and it is one of the first to conduct tests empirically and demonstrate that besides online games addiction, social media addiction is another form of Internet addiction that is pervasive among adolescents in urban China today. The study provides a comprehensive understanding of the status quo of social media addiction as a social phenomenon among adolescents—its sociopsychological antecedents, gratifications-obtained, and impact on academic performance and social capital. In addition to creating the social media addiction index, this study goes beyond the level of addiction and identifies four social media addiction symptoms that adolescents experience, thus complementing existing media addiction research.

Secondly, this study expands the scope of U&G research. It demonstrates how the U&G approach is capable of, to a certain extent, explaining media addiction. Results revealed the relationship between gratifications and media addiction that when functional alternatives are limited and adolescents constantly seek sensations especially entertainment gratifications to satisfy their psychological needs, addiction ensues. Entertainment gratifications are more likely than social and information gratifications to lead to media addiction. In addition, this study further established the mediation effects of gratifications acting between sociopsychological traits and social media addiction. It supplements the U&G approach by proposing that, if people with certain sociopsychological traits can be largely satisfied by media use, they are very likely to become media addicts. Furthermore, this study consolidates the previous gratification dimensions of social media and provides an integrated understanding of social media gratifications as a whole. It also complements the traditional inventory of media gratifications by identifying kinds of gratifications that are unique to social media, such as social exchange and peer attention, which emphasize the social functions of social media.

Thirdly, this study also contributes to the media effects tradition by exploring not only the possible effects of the new media on people in terms of satisfying their social and psychological needs but also the possible negative effects due to heavy use of the new kinds of media.

Fourthly, this study provides preliminary findings to demonstrate how sociopsychological traits relate to social media addiction. It can be helpful for psychologists to examine further the underlying psychological or biological mechanism of social media addiction, so that effective treatments and interventions can be devised to target coping with social media addiction.

Finally, this study provides a comprehensive picture of the current status of social media addiction in the Chinese context. As social media have become overwhelmingly popular around the world, many western scholars may have also begun to pay attention to the overuse of social media in their countries. The findings of this study can be used for cross-cultural comparisons, which is beneficial for further understanding of the effects of social media in different cultural contexts.

8.2.2 Practical Implications: To Parents

This study cautions parents that social media addiction is indeed a problem existing among adolescents, which can impair their academic performance and social capital. It suggests that parents need to make efforts to prevent adolescents from social media addiction.

Parents of net generation now face a common challenge: social media, which adolescents often use to communicate with friends online, alienate the parents from the interpersonal networks of adolescents. In former times without the Internet, parents knew the kinds of offline activities that their sons or daughters participated in and with whom they associated. However, in the Internet era, the net generation knows more about the new communication technologies than their parents. It is likely that parents not only do not know with whom adolescents interact online but also cannot figure out what they are doing exactly with social media. Therefore, parents should stay updated and watch over the contents that adolescents exchange with their peers via social media.

It is difficult for parents to control their sons and daughters during the adolescent years. This study demonstrated a vicious circle in which, on one hand, parents have more control over adolescents who are not self-disciplined enough. However, in this scenario, the stricter the parental control on social media use, the stronger the likelihood of addiction. On the other hand, the more severe the addiction and symptoms, the stricter the parental control of social media use. Rosen (2007) pointed out that for parents of adolescents preoccupied by the Internet, simply removing the computer or Internet connection is overwhelming because it antagonizes the adolescents and encourages them to figure out how to get online elsewhere. Adolescents are rebellious and want to be independent. They do not want to share their social media content with their parents. They set private passwords for their QQ and blogs, do not want to add their parents as friends in SNS, and so on. Thus, restrictive parental control may not work well. Previous research suggested that participative and supportive parental monitoring can largely decrease the probability of adolescents' Internet addiction (Leung and Lee 2012; Lin et al. 2009), while authoritarian parenting style can easily trigger rebellious behaviors and thus may result in counteraction (Tao et al. 2007; Zhao 2010). To prevent adolescents from escaping their problems and worries through excessive social media use, a major action that parents can take is to provide harmonious family environments for them. Parents should consistently encourage their sons or daughters, no matter how well or poorly they perform in school. If the parent-child relationship is supportive enough, adolescents are less likely to turn to other channels to relieve pressures or seek recognition.

IM is the most popular social medium among adolescents. This study demonstrates that the overuse of IM in particular is likely to have a negative impact on the academic performance of adolescents. Therefore, parents should pay special attention to adolescents' IM use. Adolescents should not be allowed to do homework next to computers with IM on in the background at all times. Instead, parents can let them use IM to chat with friends for a while to relax after they finish doing homework. Although parents are advised to respect adolescents' privacy, they still need to watch over the content that adolescents transmit through IM and with whom they communicate in IM. Parents should make sure that their children do not use IM to exchange homework answers and are not involved in online love relationships or pornography, which may not only impair their academic performance but also harm their personal development. Since this study shows that the excessive use of IM, SNS, blogs, and microblogs can all result in addiction, parents and adolescents can negotiate an agreement on the appropriate amount of time spent on social media every day. Rosen (2007) suggested that creating a behavioral contract might be helpful, in which parents stipulate the expected limitation of Internet behavior and usage time and the positive and negative consequences if adolescents do or do not obey.

This study revealed that adolescents who are leisurely bored are more likely to be addicted to social media, show various addiction symptoms, and further suffer from decreases in academic performance. Therefore, parents should encourage adolescents to participate in more offline social activities and arrange weekend family outdoor activities, such as climbing hills, playing sports, or riding bicycles. Lin et al. (2009) also suggested in their study among Taiwan adolescents that family outdoor activities would decrease the probability of adolescents' Internet addiction. Meanwhile, parents should encourage adolescents to foster their hobbies and help them to discover their own interest and potential in order to avoid leisure boredom.

Furthermore, parents are advised not to place the computer in the adolescent's private room but in an open place at home. Rosen (2007) cautioned parents that placing computers in the adolescent's room might be a precursor to Internet addiction. If adolescents can use the computer privately, they would have free rein to use social media. They consider parents opening their door and checking what they are doing on the computer as offending their privacy. Placing the computer in an open place not only allows parents to monitor the online behavior of the adolescents but also makes adolescents more self-disciplined. If setting up the computer in a common area at home is impossible, parents at least need to adopt an "open door policy," that is, whenever adolescents are on the computer, the door must be open (Rosen 2007).

Finally, this study found that mobile phones facilitate adolescents' social media addiction. It is not necessary for parents to buy mobile phones for their children. Parents should consider simple mobile phones without Internet connection functions for their children in order to prevent mobile QQ use both in class and after lights out. Adolescents often are not self-disciplined, so these are ways to stop misuse of social media at the origin.

8.2.3 Practical Implications: To Educators

This study also provides educators with a comprehensive picture of social media addiction problems among adolescents. Moreover, it calls for the attention and proper intervention of educators to the problem.

Social media can act as an online channel for teachers to interact with students outside the classroom. Teachers can set up QQ groups and thus learn more about the current feelings and thoughts of students on their online spaces. If adolescents appear troubled and confused in their online spaces, then teachers should try to help them out. Since the excessive use of IM leads to a high probability of damaging the academic performance of adolescents, teachers can also detect the abuse of IM among students through QQ groups. If a teacher notices that a certain student appears online during class time or very late at night in the class QQ group, that student may have high tendency to addiction. The teacher then should provide proper guidance to correct the inappropriate social media use of that student at an early stage.

Adolescents who are good at impression management in social media tend to be addicted, especially those who often make excuses for not getting good grades or for being blamed by teachers. It is possible that adolescents who do not perform well at school are not recognized or praised by teachers often enough. Thus, these students may turn to social media for attention and recognition. Therefore, teachers and educators should try to find the strengths of the students, encourage them, and provide care and guidance, particularly to those who do not perform well in their studies but have a strong need for recognition. If students have enough attention and recognition offline, it is less likely that they will seek it online.

Because this study indicates that information seeking and friendship maintenance through social media are not likely to lead to addiction but can help to improve students' academic performance, teachers can encourage these functions. Students can be encouraged to make good use of the social media, for information seeking and sharing, group discussions, and cooperative learning, which may be beneficial for their studies. However, if teachers notice that some students use social media instead of what they should be doing or to escape from their study tasks, teachers should provide directions to prevent them from addiction.

Adolescents are always full of spirit. As mentioned above, adolescents who experience leisure boredom tend to be addicted to social media. Sufficient group activities may enrich adolescents' lives after class and prevent them from Internet addiction (Tao et al. 2007). Thus, schools are recommended to arrange various kinds of extracurricular activities for students, as well as offline social activities or hobby groups for students during summer and winter holidays. These can provide more opportunities for students to both socialize with each other and foster hobbies. Since loss of interest in offline social activities is a symptom of addiction, if teachers find that a certain student is often inactive and not interested in participating in offline social activities, they should pay attention to that student's online behavior.

Furthermore, to prevent the abuse of social media via mobile phones, schools should have strict rules regarding mobile phone use on campus. Strict rules, an encouraging learning environment, supportive teacher guidance, as well as rich and colorful extracurricular activities can lead adolescents to enjoy their campus life and largely prevent them from social media addiction.

8.3 Limitations and Suggestions for Future Research

Research is never perfect, and the present study is no exception. Although this study was carefully designed and executed, the following limitations exist.

First, this study employed a cross-sectional design. Despite its large sample size of more than 1,500 cases, which is a rich pool of data appropriate for sophisticated statistical analysis, it was not sufficient to establish causal relationships. A panel study in a longitudinal design is encouraged in the future to compare the results from the same sample at different time intervals and to accumulate a more intensive understanding of social media addiction among adolescents.

Second, the middle schools selected from five cities were not totally random. The schools that participated in the survey were those who were willing to participate. This is understandable because in the past many schools were requested to take part in illegitimate or unprofessional research and now have very strict rules forbidding any kind of survey. Furthermore, in 2010, several notorious cases occurred successively and severely damaged school security in China, which attracted much attention from both government and society. Consequently, especially at the end of 2010 when the surveys were conducted, many schools still did not allow outsiders to get in. Getting permission to execute surveys in schools is always a difficulty for researchers.

Third, this study is an exploratory research. In factor analysis, the eigenvalues of some factors are less than 1, and the Cronbach's alpha of certain measures are less than desirable. The scale used for measuring the level of use is not truly interval. It is because the study would like to measure the normal social media use and at the same time differentiate the addictive use. Future research should be able to improve these statistical results and consider using a more stringent interval scale.

Fourth, the four social media addiction symptoms identified in this research are unlikely to be exhaustive. Future research should explore more possible symptoms of social media addiction that adolescents experience. Future research can consider using a more stringent criterion to classify social media addicts, so as to identify the extreme cases and examine them further in details. Other possible sociopsychological antecedents of social media addiction, such as procrastination and affinity seeking, can be tested in future research. Moreover, as Livingstone and Helsper (2010) called for balancing opportunities and risks in adolescents' use of the Internet, future study should also examine other possible effects, particularly the positive influence of social media on users, such as improvement in online interpersonal communication competence.

Fifth, the parental control measured in this study might be related to parents' level of computer knowledge. It is likely that some parents do want to control their children's computer use but they are not able to. Future research can investigate further the relationships among parental control, parents' level of computer knowledge, and adolescents' social media addiction.

Finally, as social media are overwhelmingly popular among netizens in recent years, social media addiction may be a phenomenon among not only adolescents but also college students, white-collar and blue-collar workers, and so on. Future studies can focus on these groups. Future research should also consider conducting similar investigations in rural areas in order to compare the differences in social media usage patterns between rural areas and urban cities in China. Furthermore, future research should aim at providing practical guidance and intervention for the reduction of social media addiction among not only adolescents but also other age groups.

References

American Psychiatric Association. (1994). *Diagnostic and statistical manual for mental disorders* (4th ed.). Washington, DC: American Psychiatric Association.

Cao, F., & Su, L. (2007). Internet addiction among Chinese adolescents: Prevalence and psychological features. *Child: Care, Health & Development, 33*(3), 275–281.

Chak, K., & Leung, L. (2004). Shyness and locus of control as predictors of Internet addiction and Internet use. *CyberPsychology & Behavior, 7*(5), 559–570.

Chen, G. M. (2011). Tweet this: A uses and gratifications perspective on how active Twitter use gratifies a need to connect with others. *Computers in Human Behavior, 27*(2), 755–762.

Cheuk, W. S., & Chan, Z. C. Y. (2007). ICQ (I Seek You) and adolescents: A quantitative study in Hong Kong. *CyberPsychology & Behavior, 10*(1), 108–114.

Cheung, L. M., & Wong, W. S. (2011). The effects of insomnia and Internet addiction on depression in Hong Kong adolescents: An exploratory cross-sectional analysis. *Journal of Sleep Research, 20*(2), 311–317.

Cheung, C. M., Chiu, P. Y., & Lee, M. K. (2011). Online social networks: Why do students use facebook? *Computers in Human Behavior, 27*, 1337–1343.

CNNIC. (2011). *The 27th statistical survey report on Internet development in China.* Retrieved April 20, 2011, from http://www.cnnic.net.cn/dtygg/dtgg/201101/P020110119328960192287.pdf

Cohen, D. T. (2007, August). *Building social capital through online communities: The strategy of Ned Lamont's 2006 senate campaign.* Paper presented at the annual meeting of American Political Science Association, Chicago, IL, USA.

Comm, J. (2010). *Twitter power 2.0: How to dominate your market one tweet at a time.* Hoboken: Wiley.

Dunne, A., & Lawlor, M. (2010). Young people's use of online social networking sites—A uses and gratifications perspective. *Journal of Research in Interactive Marketing, 4*(1), 46–58.

Elliott, R., Eccles, S., & Gournay, K. (1996). Revenge, existential choice, and addictive consumption. *Psychology and Marketing, 13*, 753–768.

Ellison, N., Steinfield, C., & Lampe, C. (2007). The benefits of Facebook "friends": Exploring the relationship between college students' use of online social networks and social capital. *Journal of Computer-Mediated Communication, 12*(4), 1143–1168.

Ellison, N., Steinfield, C., & Lampe, C. (2009, May). *Connection strategies: Relationship formation and maintenance on social network sites.* Paper presented at the annual meeting of the International Communication Association, Chicago, IL, USA.

Fallows, D. (2007). *Internet addiction in China.* Retrieved May 15, 2011, from http://www.pewinternet.org/Commentary/2007/September/Internet-Addiction-in-China.aspx

Geng, Y., Su, L., & Cao, F. (2006). A research on emotion and personality characteristics in junior 1 high school students with Internet addiction disorders. *Chinese Journal of Clinical Psychology, 14*, 153–155.

Ghassemzadeh, L., Shahraray, M., & Moradi, A. (2008). Prevalence of Internet addiction and comparison of Internet addicts and non-addicts in Iranian high schools. *CyberPsychology & Behavior, 11*(6), 731–733.

Gong, J., Chen, X., Zeng, J., Li, F., Zhou, D., & Wang, Z. (2009). Adolescent addictive Internet use and drug abuse in Wuhan, China. *Addiction Research & Theory, 17*(3), 291–305.

Hindman, M. S. (2007). *Voice, equality, and the Internet.* Retrieved July 10, 2011, from http://files.uniteddiversity.com/Decision_Making_and_Democracy/voice_equality_and_the_internet.pdf

Homans, G. C. (1958). Social behavior as exchange. *American Journal of Sociology, 63*(6), 597–606.

Huang, H. (2008, July). *Instant messenger use among teenagers in China: Motives, shyness, alienation, and social support.* Paper presented at the annual conference of International Association for Media and Communication Research Conference, Stockholm, Sweden.

Huang, H., & Leung, L. (2009). Instant messaging addiction among teenagers in China: Shyness, alienation, and academic performance decrement. *CyberPsychology & Behavior, 12*(6), 675–679.

Huang, L., Chou, Y., & Lin, C. (2008). In influence of reading motives on the responses after reading blogs. *CyberPsychology & Behavior, 11*(3), 351–355.

Hwang, H. (2009, May). *Predictors of instant messaging: Gratifications sought, gratifications obtained, and social presence.* Paper presented at the annual meeting of the International Communication Association, New York City, NY, USA.

Iso-Ahola, S. E., & Weissinger, E. (1990). Perceptions of boredom in leisure: Conceptualization, reliability and validity of the leisure boredom scale. *Journal of Leisure Research, 22*(1), 1–17.

Johnson, P. R., & Yang, S. (2009, August). *Uses and gratifications of Twitter: An examination of users' motives and satisfaction of Twitter use.* Paper presented at the communication technology division of the annual convention of the Association for Education in Journalism and Mass Communication, Boston, MA, USA.

Jung, T., Youn, H., & McClung, S. (2007). Motivations and self-presentation strategies on Korean-based "Cyworld" weblog format personal homepages. *CyberPsychology & Behavior, 10*(1), 24–31.

Kerr, J. (2009, April). *Surging together: A preliminary inquiry into the effects of Internet use on social capital in American communities.* Paper presented at the annual meeting of Midwestern Political Science Association, Chicago, IL, USA.

Ko, H., & Kuo, F. (2009). Can blogging enhance subjective well-being through self-disclosure? *CyberPsychology & Behavior, 12*(1), 75–79.

Ko, C. H., Yen, J. Y., Yen, C. F., Lin, H. C., & Yang, M. J. (2007). Factors predictive for incidence and remission of Internet addiction in young adolescents: A prospective study. *CyberPsychology & Behavior, 10*(4), 545–551.

Ko, C. H., Yen, J. Y., Yen, C. F., Chen, C. S., Weng, C. C., & Chen, C. C. (2008). The association between Internet addiction and problematic alcohol use in adolescents: The problem behavior model. *CyberPsychology & Behavior, 11*(5), 571–576.

Kramer, N. C., & Winter, S. (2008). Impression management 2.0. The relationship of self-esteem, extraversion, self-efficacy, and self-presentation within social network sites. *Journal of Media Psychology, 20*(3), 106–116.

Lam, L., Peng, Z., Mai, J., & Jing, J. (2009). Factors associated with Internet addiction among adolescents. *CyberPsychology & Behavior, 12*(5), 551–555.

Leary, M. R. (1996). *Self-presentation: Impression management and interpersonal behavior.* Boulder: Westview Press.

Lee, D., Im, S., & Taylor, C. (2008). Voluntary self-disclosure of information on the Internet: A multimethod study of the motivations and consequences of disclosing information on blogs. *Psychology & Marketing, 25*(7), 692–710.

Leung, L. (2001). College student motives for chatting on ICQ. *New Media & Society, 3*(4), 483–500.

Leung, L. (2008). Leisure boredom, sensation seeking, self-esteem, addiction symptoms and patterns of mobile phone use. In E. Korini, S. Utz, M. Tanis, & S. B. Barnes (Eds.), *Mediated interpersonal communication.* New York: Routledge.

Leung, L. (2009). Users-generated content on the Internet: An examination of gratifications, civic engagement, and psychological empowerment. *New Media & Society, 11*(8), 1327–1347.

Leung, L., & Lee, P. S. N. (2012). The influences of information literacy, Internet addiction and parenting styles on Internet risks. *New Media & Society, 14*, 117–136.

Li, X., Li, Z., & Xie, W. (2006). Epidemiological investigation on Internet addiction among middle school students in Hefei. *Chinese Mental Health Journal, 20*, 51–54.

Li, C., Liu, J., Guo, S., Zhang, W., Fang, Z., & Jiang, H. (2009). Analyses of Internet use among college students. *Journal of Dalian University of Technology (Social Sciences), 30*(3), 104–107.

Lin, C. H., & Yu, S. F. (2008). Adolescent Internet usage in Taiwan: Exploring gender differences. *Adolescence, 43*(170), 317–331.

Lin, C., Lin, S., & Wu, C. (2009). The effects of parental monitoring and leisure boredom on adolescents' Internet addiction. *Adolescence, 44*(176), 993–1004.

Liu, Y. (2007). Psycho-social related factors of junior high school students with Internet addiction disorder. *Chinese Journal of Clinical Psychology, 15*, 422–423.

Livingstone, S., & Helsper, E. (2010). Balancing opportunities and risks in teenagers' use of the Internet: The role of online skills and Internet self-efficacy. *New Media & Society, 12*(2), 309–329.

Ljungstrand, P., & Segestad, Y. H. (2000). Awareness of presence, instant messaging and webwho. *Siggroup Bulletin, 21*(3), 21–27.

Lu, H. P., Lin, C. C., Hsiao, K. L., & Cheng, L. T. (2010). Information sharing behavior on blogs in Taiwan: Effects of interactivities and gender differences. *Journal of Information Science, 36*(3), 401–416.

Martinez, H. (2009, January 23). Tweet this: Southeast Texans microblog every day happenings and more. *Beaumont Enterprise.*

Murray, H. A. (1938). *Explorations in personality*. New York: Oxford University Press.

Nalwa, K., & Anand, A. P. (2003). Internet addiction in students: A cause of concern. *CyberPsychology & Behavior, 6*(6), 653–656.

Odaci, H., & Kalkan, M. (2010). Problematic Internet use, loneliness and dating anxiety among young adult university students. *Computers & Education, 55*(3), 1091–1097.

Park, N., Kee, K. F., & Valenzuela, S. (2009). Being immersed in social networking environment: Facebook groups, uses and gratifications, and social outcomes. *CyberPsychology & Behavior, 12*(6), 729–733.

Quan-Haase, A., & Young, A. L. (2010). Bulletin of science. *Technology & Society, 30*(5), 350–361.

Raacke, J., & Bonds-Raacke, J. (2008). MySpace and Facebook: Applying the uses and gratifications theory to exploring friend-networking sites. *CyberPsychology & Behavior, 11*(2), 169–174.

Ramirez, A., Dimmick, J., Feaster, J., & Lin, S. (2008). Revisiting interpersonal media competition—The gratification niches of instant messaging, email, and the telephone. *Communication Research, 35*(4), 529–547.

Recchiuti, J. K. (2003). *College students' uses and motives for email, instant messaging, and online chat rooms.* Unpublished master's thesis. University of Delaware, Newark, DE, USA.

Rosen, L. D. (2007). *Me, MySpace, and I: Parenting the net generation.* New York: Palgrave Macmillan.

Song, I., LaRose, R., Eastin, M. S., & Lin, C. A. (2004). Internet gratifications and Internet addiction: On the uses and abuses of new media. *CyberPsychology & Behavior, 7*(4), 384–394.

Steinfield, C., Ellison, N., & Lampe, C. (2008). Social capital, self-esteem, and use of online social network sites: A longitudinal analysis. *Journal of Applied Developmental Psychology, 29*(6), 434–445.

Steinfield, C., DiMicco, J. M., Ellison, N. B., & Lampe, C. (2009). Bowling online: Social networking and social capital within the organization. In *Proceedings of the fourth international conference on communities and technologies* (pp. 245–254). New York: ACM.

Sun, S. J., Rubin, A. M., & Haridakis, P. M. (2006, June). *The role of motivation and media involvement in explaining Internet dependency.* Paper presented at the International Communication Association Annual Conference, Dresden, Germany.

Tao, R., Ying, L., Yue, X., & Hao, X. (2007). *Internet addiction: Exploration and interventions.* Shanghai: Century Publishing Group.

Trammell, K. D., Tarkowski A., & Hofmokl, J. (2004, September). *Republic of blog.* Paper presented at the 5th annual meeting of the Association of Internet Researchers, Brighton, UK.

Tsai, C. C., & Lin, S. J. (2003). Internet addiction of adolescents in Taiwan: An interview study. *CyberPsychology & Behavior, 6*, 649–652.

Twenge, J. M., & Campbell, W. K. (2009). *The narcissism epidemic: Living in the age of entitlement.* New York: Free Press.

Urista, M. A., Dong, Q., & Day, K. D. (2009). Explaining why young adults use MySpace and Facebook through uses and gratification theory. *Human Communication, 12*(2), 215–229.

Wang, Y., & Fesenmaier, D. (2004). Modeling participation in an online travel community. *Journal of Travel Research, 42*, 261–270.

Wang, H., & Yu, Z. (2006). The characteristics of Internet and its cause to adolescents' delinquency. *Journal of Jilin Public Security Academy, 21*(3), 41–54.

Wu, Z. (2007). *Why family can hurt people—Disclose the psychological truth in family.* Shanghai: World Publishing Corporation.

Yang, S. C., & Tung, C. J. (2007). Comparison of Internet addicts and non-addicts in Taiwanese high school. *Computer in Human Behavior, 23*(1), 79–96.

Young, K. S. (1999). Internet addiction: Symptoms, evaluation, and treatment. In L. VandeCreek & T. Jackson (Eds.), *Innovations in clinical practice: A source book* (Vol. 17, pp. 19–31). Sarasota: Professional Resource Press.

Yuen, C. N., & Lavin, M. J. (2004). Internet dependence in the collegiate population: The role of shyness. *CyberPsychology & Behavior, 7*(4), 379–383.

Zhang, Y., & Hu, J. (2010). The impact of Internet culture on college students' interpersonal competence. *Economic and Social Development, 8*(6), 177–179.

Zhao, C. (2010). *Children beside windows: The family factors of game addiction*. Hangzhou: Zhejiang University Press.

MIX
Papier aus verantwortungsvollen Quellen
Paper from responsible sources
FSC® C105338

If you have any concerns about our products,
you can contact us on
ProductSafety@springernature.com

In case Publisher is established outside the EU,
the EU authorized representative is:
Springer Nature Customer Service Center GmbH
Europaplatz 3, 69115 Heidelberg, Germany

Printed by Libri Plureos GmbH
in Hamburg, Germany